EARLY AMERICAN
DECORATION

EARLY AMERICAN DECORATION

A Comprehensive Treatise

Revealing the technique involved in the art of early American decoration of furniture, walls, tinware, etc.

❡An invaluable reference book and a complete course of instruction for the student of early design and restoration

By ESTHER STEVENS BRAZER

Illustrated from drawings and natural-color photographs by the Author

PUBLISHED BY
THE POND-EKBERG COMPANY
SPRINGFIELD, MASSACHUSETTS

THIRD PRINTING, 1950
PRINTED IN THE UNITED STATES OF AMERICA
BY THE PUBLISHERS

TO MY HUSBAND
BY WHOSE FAITH, INSPIRATION AND GUIDANCE
THIS BOOK HAS BEEN MOULDED

In Memoriam

IN THE PASSING ON OCTOBER 30, 1945 OF

ESTHER STEVENS BRAZER

ALL THOSE INTERESTED IN THE STUDY
OF EARLY AMERICAN DECORATION LOST
THE LEADING AUTHORITY OF HER TIME,
AN ENTHUSIASTIC AND SYMPATHETIC
TEACHER WHOSE RARE GIFTS AS A BRIGHT
COLORIST WITH DEXTEROUS SKILL AND
AUTHENTIC ACCURACY WERE AN INSPI-
RATION TO ALL WHO CAME IN
CONTACT WITH HER

This book is her monument

Author's Foreword

EARLY in my study of old-time painted designs, it became apparent that the processes used in decorating antique furniture and tinware were of a different nature than those now commonly employed. Diligent search of practical books failed to reveal any information on the subject, and teachers in this line were not available. It therefore became necessary for me to learn by analytical observation of the designs themselves, through attempting to record the exact effects, and by tracking down odd bits of information in some antique instruction book. Not since 1825 has a decorative painter's guide appeared upon the market, and many are the claims that stenciling and gold-leaf work have become "forgotten arts."

Learning by trial-and-error methods was so costly in time and effort that I now make bold to present the results of my research in the hope that craftsmen who wish to restore old designs may know how to execute them. It is my earnest wish that antique furniture and tinware, old-time decorated walls and floors, may be restored with their proper designs and with their own methods of painting. If, by broadcasting knowledge of old patterns and the ways to restore them, I may succeed in causing some examples now in damaged form to be rescued from oblivion, I shall count my effort well expended. Our old-time designers had a feeling for beauty which we would do well to follow, and a love of color we may employ enthusiastically today.

·   ·   ·

In presenting the following information, I wish to make it clear that this work has been a highly coöperative venture. I am deeply indebted to the kindness of antique collectors and dealers who so generously allowed me to study, photograph and otherwise record designs they had in their possession. Among these, none is more prominent than Mrs. Arthur Oldham, whose collection of decorated pieces covers a varied and extensive field. Also, I am grateful to my students for the patterns they found on furniture and tinware, and allowed me to add to our collective fund of knowledge. We have all worked together in a common cause — the preserving and renewing of an art that was rapidly falling into oblivion. To all these helpers I wish to express my deepest appreciation and sincerest thanks.

ESTHER STEVENS BRAZER

"INNERWYCK"
Flushing, New York City

···◦[x]◦···

CONTENTS

CONTENTS *(Continued)*

⤛❦⤜

ILLUSTRATIONS

Color Plates in Demonstration Section

EARLY AMERICAN
DECORATION

The Historical Background of Decorative Design

LOVE of ornament and color is as old as civilization. Man, when he first emerged from savage state, made use of incised lines or colored designs to ornament household implements. Walls of prehistoric caves in Spain are adorned with painted animals in action, surprisingly well portrayed for their primitive period. Egyptian tombs and temples, following the custom of native palaces, have painted walls still bright with representations of religious rites or military exploits. So through Greek and Roman days, color adorned many sculptured pediments, heroic statues of gods, and walls of temples. The painted plaster walls of Pompeiian homes show the wealth of color and artistic achievement characteristic of that age. Even during Gothic times, when carving was carried to such a high point of perfection, color was still employed to enhance its richness, while colorful diaper patterns and borders were used on otherwise plain surfaces. Then came the Renaissance with its classic feeling for simple beauty bringing into being some of the most famous examples of painted ornament. Beginning in Italy, this glorious art spread into France, England and Northern Europe when various patrons of art imported Italian masters of outstanding merit into their own countries.

In England, however, color received a serious setback during the Reformation. Religious fanatics caused the finest and most gorgeous examples of Gothic art to be destroyed, so that our knowledge of color in this period is most fragmentary. The Reformed church decreed that statues be destroyed, color and gilding be removed, illuminated books and manuscripts be burned, along with playing-cards and other gaming devices. Decorated walls were covered over with drab paint, and England went into a temporary dark age of its own.

Such was the background which surrounded those early groups of courageous and adventurous Englishmen who journeyed forth to this new world where a new history was to be made and written. Here they must meet the urgent problem of providing food and shelter, a struggle which occupied all their available energy for the first few decades. Then, as the rigors of existence abated, and the Puritan religion became more liberal in its rigid doctrine against artistic adornment, our settlers began to enrich their domestic surroundings. Certain artisans could fashion carved chests, others made use of paint to decorate various kinds of furniture. Painted decoration could be achieved as quickly as any type of ornament, and pigments were obtainable from natural products or by importation. The Indians here had both red and yellow ochre which are earthen deposits; lamp black could be compounded from the soot in any chimney; verdigris, the basis of early green paint, could be scraped from old copper. Prussian blue was manufactured from the blood of slaughtered animals. Whiting was easily imported, and other colors were brought over as trade with the old country increased by leaps and bounds. A process for making white lead may have been used here at an early date. With two or three of these pigments, our old-time decorator could achieve strikingly effective ornament, if his ability and training were sufficient.

The earliest use of paint in this country was on furniture, where a small amount of pigment went a long way. When, in the early 1700's, the preservative qualities of paint began to dawn upon our ancestors, they made use of it to protect interior woodwork and wall surfaces as well as all wood exposed to the weather. That is, those who were thrifty took care of their property by painting. Some pigments seem to have had a higher resistance to exposure than others, particularly the old-time white lead prepared by a slow and laborious process not used today. Two signboards, long exposed to merciless rains and frosts, remain indelibly in my memory. One is a weather-beaten board which was formerly at the entrance to a toll road, listing the various prices charged for man, vehicle, and beast. The background was never painted, but the lettering and prices were painted once in black, and once in dark red. The unprotected background was worn away at least a sixteenth of an inch, leaving the lettering in distinct bas-relief, as if woodcarving had been resorted to. The other signboard hung for years outside the Indian King Tavern at Haddonfield, New Jersey. On its reverse there had been painted a bald eagle with head and outstretched wings against a glorious sunburst. All traces of paint are gone, but in a strong light this design can be seen in faintest relief. Where the decorator superimposed two or more paints the wood stands up more boldly in contrast to the background, sculptured by Father Time. I have often wondered how it happens that, in this modern day of "Save-the-surface-and-you-save-all" campaigns, paint manufacturers have never exploited one of these signboards.

The extent of painted furniture in this country must have been far more widespread than the few examples which now survive. We may reckon on many that have been destroyed by fire, many that have been chopped up for kindling (as some of us can testify by oft-told family history), many that have been repainted so that the original design is not visible, and many that have had their painted finish scraped down to the natural wood. Throughout all the New England colonies, New York, New Jersey, and Pennsylvania, the custom of decorating furniture was much employed. But through Virginia, Maryland, and the more southern colonies we find fewer examples of furniture made and decorated on native soil, and most of these are post-Revolutionary in date. Prior to that time, these Southern colonies were closely bound by active trade with their mother countries, and the fine homes of these regions were adorned mostly with furniture from England, France and Spain. Local products were not fine enough for the mansion houses of Virginia, Louisiana, or South Carolina.

A greater stretch of the imagination is required to guess the extent to which early pine floors were ornamented with painted designs. I personally believe that after the Revolution the decoration of floors in "best" rooms was usual when carpeting and fine rugs were not available. But painted floors wear out so rapidly and are repainted so constantly, that few remain to tell us of their existence. Now and then, straw matting is removed from the floor of a long-disused room, or an old carpet is taken up, and there lies revealed evidence of a most unexpected design. If it were possible to persuade more people to scrape away outer coats of paint, in search of a decoration, I am sure that we would find many more examples than have come to light at the present time. Housewives of those days had just as keen an interest in beautifying their homes as they have today, and the itinerant decorator was easily available when home talent was insufficient.

As for the painted walls that became popular when wallpaper came into style here around 1760, there is no telling how far and wide this custom spread. Remote sections of the country where wallpaper was not easily obtainable, were scoured by artisans of more or less ability eager to fresco walls with small patterns, or with large landscapes like the French scenic papers imported by the wealthy. Many houses so decorated have fallen prey to fire or decay, others have had the designs papered over because they were not in perfect condition, or did not conform to the owner's taste in interior decoration. Now we must travel on remote, grass-grown roads outside of quiet New England villages to see such walls in untouched condition, or to gather tracings of designs that remain in fragmentary form. Close to pioneer life these patterned walls clung, evidence of the universal love of color and ornament, no matter how drab the hard work of a farm might be. We hear of other stenciled walls in northern New York state, in southern Pennsylvania, and even in Ohio where one of the first taverns in the Western Reserve is still standing.

Unfortunately, the identity of those who painted American furniture in olden times has seldom been recorded. We would like to know more about the men, or women, who ornamented the pieces which have long outlived their memory. We want to know something about their life and experiences, their hardships and their pleasures. But only a few fleeting glimpses of these craftsmen are obtainable, and these are largely impressions or deductions, rather than facts. Many a decorator have I pursued in the hope of finding something of human interest, yet even when I find his name, the evidence is inconclusive and his personality elusive. Many of the decorators were a bit impractical, and traveled from place to place working for their board and lodging, seldom marrying and establishing a home. Mostly, we must know them by their works, letting the products of their craftsmanship speak for them.

Our earliest painted chests were undoubtedly ornamented by the joiners who constructed them from first to last. In the period which preceded the 18th century, various trades and crafts were not so highly individualized as later. The early joiner made both houses and furniture, carved them or painted them according to his ability. After 1750, at least in the larger cities, we often find the trade of carver differentiated from that of joiner, cabinetmaker from that of chairmaker, and so on. Then the painting of furniture may have become somewhat divorced from its construction, for artists, sign painters and picture-frame makers began to decorate furniture and mirrors. Coach painters had every qualification for decorating furniture, and their ability to do fine striping may account for the prominence of this accent on pieces of post-Revolutionary date. Shops turning out rush, cane and wood seat chairs may have employed their own painter to finish them — perhaps one of those coach painters out of work in the post-war depression. House painters may have ventured into the decoration of furniture on a less elaborate scale, as they undoubtedly essayed the ornamentation of paneling and floors. Then there were the tinware manufacturers who turned out large quantities of ornamental tin from 1780 on. Whoever decorated tin trays and boxes may have painted chairs and other pieces of furniture, for there is no telling where a man who can wield brush and paint will stop! In Berlin, Connecticut, where the tin industry was first established in America, it is said that Hiram Mygatt, "an ornamental coach painter," had a shop at the rear of his premises for the japanning of tinware.

Curiously enough, up to the close of the Revolution, we have no evidence that women painted a single piece of American furniture. Angelica Kauffmann seems to have led off with the honors in England about 1760, and shortly thereafter we begin to find an occasional American piece that appears to have been decorated by a courageous young lady on this side of the Atlantic. Women, previously, had been too much occupied with the cares of a household, with the many crafts required in spinning, weaving, sewing and candlemaking. But weaving mills were being established; shipping on an extensive scale brought to her door many products which were not available before; slaves lessened the demand on the housewife's time. The polite education of young ladies at boarding school had been fostered, and painting had crept into the curriculum of such educational establishments. While the merits of needlework and embroidery were still extolled, the art of "theorem painting" (where pictures were copied by means of stencils) and velvet painting were far more popular. Thus we find that a young lady educated in such arts would occasionally decorate her sewing table or writing box, revealing her lack of trade experience by her omission of striping, and by the infinitesimal labor devoted to the decorative design. In time, however, young ladies not too well blessed with worldly goods learned to do the professional decorator's task with swift sure brush stroke, and painted chairs, tinware, and other articles as a means of livelihood.

Thus it appears that subsequent to 1800, masculine decorators were forced to accept feminine competition in their trade. Hitchcock is said to have used women for the application of stencil designs between 1826 and 1839 when his factory in Hitchcocksville failed for the second time. Nowadays we find a preponderance of women in this trade which once was so exclusively masculine.

In our study of painting methods, it has not been deemed necessary to draw a line of distinction between the processes used in this country and those employed in England and on the Continent. The more we learn through research about the skill of early American craftsmen, the more we feel that they matched the work of old-world artisans. If Paul Revere was interested in fostering the industry of manufacturing painted trays and tin-ware, using his English-trained nephew-in-law as foreman, and his nephew as decorator, there is likely to be little difference between their product and the finer trays made in Wales. We know that Revere imported an exten-sive shipment of "Roman" (meaning decorated in the Pompeiian style) tea trays and waiters in the ship *Broad Oak* out of Bristol, England, in 1783. There has long been a tradition that lace-edge trays were Revere trays, and we well know the pierced tin lanterns called by his name. If, then, our local craftsmen were making such fine tinware in the early days of the industry, there is no reason why we could not have been making subse-quently all the other forms known to have been made in the mother country. Of the painting methods described in this volume, the obscure and difficult art of "floating color" may have been most frequently used by the best japanners in England, but there is little doubt that it appears in one form or another on a few of our finest decorated pieces.

Early American painted design has been difficult to study because a com-prehensive group of widely-scattered examples has not been made by any museum. We must be constantly traveling and observing if we hope to gather a complete picture of how our early painters adorned the furniture, walls and floors of our ancestors' homes. It is to be hoped that interest in the proper preservation of original examples will increase, and Colonial interior decoration will come into its own as a delightful background for daily living.

PART ONE

*Principles of Furniture Decorating *
Materials and Tools

Principles of Furniture Decorating: Materials and Tools

CERTAIN very definite rules underlie successful decorating of furniture, just as, indeed, they underlie all good art. Insofar as these rules were followed, our old-time decorators achieved distinction; or, failing to make use of these principles, fell short of producing perfect work. A furniture decorator must consider the four following points:

FIRST: *Decorative design must* EMPHASIZE *construction.* Panels must be carefully treated as units of importance. Drawer divisions must be considered as separate spaces. Leg and seat frame construction must be emphasized to heighten apparent strength. Mouldings, bevels or other constructed finishes cannot be ignored.

SECOND: *A design must fit the space it occupies.* This means that long narrow patterns shall be used in long narrow spaces and tall patterns on tall splats or vertical panels. An insignificant design shall not be used on a large or important space. But the decorator shall keep in mind the fact that elaborate designs require a certain amount of plain space about them to set off their beauty.

THIRD: *Distribution, emphasis, and scale must be considered.* The decoration shall be properly distributed. All of the design cannot be placed on a chair back — for instance, neglecting seat frame, legs, or front stretchers. An important decoration shall be placed in the position of *importance,* such as the top slat of a chair, front face of a teapot, or panel front of a chest. Construction generally defines for us the place of importance on each piece. This position should be emphasized, in order that there be a focal point to draw the eye. The scale, or relative size, of a decoration must be suitable to the piece. It is a question of proportion: neither the furniture nor the design we place upon it must *seem dwarfed* in relationship each to the other. Thus, bold, broadly-painted designs belong on massive furniture; light, delicate patterns on refined Sheraton furniture. Too fine a pattern placed upon heavy furniture will make the pattern seem dwarfed; too bold a design upon a delicately-built piece will make the actual construction seem too small to carry such a design. The experienced decorator feels scale by instinct just as an architect knows when all elements of a building take their proper place. Proportional relationship (which is just another term for scale) must be carefully balanced between each separate unit of a decoration: the design on a chair stile, or upright post, must not be coarsely built if the patterns on other parts of the same chair are small and delicate. But if all designs on one piece are carefully picked to match in a degree of coarseness or degree of fineness already determined as suitable to the construction of this piece, there will be a feeling of correct scale that is satisfying.

FOURTH: *The decorator must make use of contrast to enhance the beauty of form.* Thus light colors are most decorative against dark colors, bright colors against neutral backgrounds, and dull shades against brilliant colors. Harmonious, even-toned coloring may make a lovely picture, but the result will not be described as "highly decorative."

To these four principles we would add another, for the decorator who is restoring antiques, namely:

FIFTH: *A decoration must be suitable to the period and to the section of the country in which the antique was constructed.* Namely, early Connecticut chests shall not be painted with patterns peculiar to certain sections of Pennsylvania. Hitchcock chairs shall be stenciled, and not painted with bunches of pink roses and blue morning glories. Sheraton chairs of dainty proportions shall be given classic gold-leaf or color designs true to their early period. We should not put early japanners' designs upon late stencil-type chairs, or stencil bronze fruit upon a lace-edge tray which antedates that technique by twenty-five or fifty years. In the pursuit of knowledge concerning appropriate designs, let us make records of authentic patterns, even though fragmentary. Also let us remember that rural pieces require their ornament in country flavor, and city-made types call for designs of greater elegance and sophistication.

MATERIALS AND TOOLS

PURPOSES FOR WHICH WE USE THEM IN DECORATING

The cost of materials employed by the decorator must not be judged by the length of the list here given. As a matter of fact, these materials last an amazingly long time, and so, once the initial supply has been laid in, do not make a constant demand upon our pocketbooks. Also it is not necessary to have *all* these different materials at once, as each decorator may not decide to go into all the branches of our craft at the very beginning. Gold leaf, at three or four cents a sheet, may become expensive when used steadily; otherwise a decorator's paint bill seldom runs more than $5.00 a month. Our own labor is by far the largest item that goes into painted design work. In the following list those materials marked with a star are requisite for stenciling with bronze.

MATERIALS AND TOOLS REQUIRED

Japan Colors in Tubes —
 Dark Red
 Vermilion
 Chrome Yellow Light
 Chrome Yellow Medium
 Brilliant Green (a yellow "leaf" green)
 Coach Painter's Green (a dark blue green)
 Azure Blue
 Lamp Black

Artists' Oil Colors in Tubes —
 The Transparent Group
  * Alizarin Crimson
  * Gamboge (Yellow) or Yellow Lake
  * Prussian Blue
  * Verdigris
  Mauve
 The Partially Transparent and Opaque Group
  Phillips White
  Lamp Black or Ivory Black
  Yellow Ochre
  Burnt Sienna
  Burnt Umber

Flat White Paint, 1 pint
* Flat Black Paint, 1 pint
Asphaltum or Asphaltum Varnish, 1 pint
Turpentine, 1 quart
Raw Linseed Oil, 1 quart

* Crude Oil, 1 quart
* Pumice, 1 pound (purchased at a drug store)
  Sandpaper #00, six sheets
  Steel Wool #0, 1 pound
  Steel Wool #1 or #2, 1 pound
  Paint and Varnish Remover, 1 quart
  Alcohol, Denatured, 1 quart
* Varnish, 24-hour drying, 1 pint (not synthetic)
  Varnish, 4-hour, such as Super Valspar
* Japan Gold Size, 1 pint
  Hiburnish Bronzing Liquid, 1 pint
  Tincture of Benzoin, 1 ounce
  Carbona, Carbon tetrachloride, or other fast evaporating cleaning fluid
  Gold Leaf, deep, on Transfer Sheet, one book
  Pale, or Lemon, Gold Leaf, one book
  Silver Leaf, one book
  Aluminum Leaf, one book
* Bronze Powders, one ounce of each —
        Aluminum
        Pale Gold (fine)
        Orange Gold
        Copper Brown
        Matt Green (pale)
        Brilliant Fire
* Drapery Velour, scrap pieces
* Silk Back Velvet, scrap pieces (no rayon or cotton velvets)
  Higgins Waterproof Drawing Ink
  Crow Quill Pen
  Etching Tool
  Wax Paper, one roll
  Brushes —
        Tiny square-tipped quill brushes, ¾-inch hair
        Square-tipped show-card brushes, #6 to #9
        1- to 2-inch varnish brushes, fine quality
        Square-tipped striping brushes, smallest size with 1½-inch hairs
* Traceolene, one roll
* Architect's Tracing Linen, one yard
* Sharp-pointed Embroidery Scissors (straight blades)
  Ruler or Metal Tape Measure
  Small Metal Caps, such as those used for screw tops on medicine bottles
  A Basket, like a two-handled market basket with the cover removed

FACTS WE SHOULD KNOW ABOUT PAINTS

While space does not permit that we go into great detail concerning the chemistry of paint, it is well to keep in mind this underlying principle: the faster a paint dries the less durable it is; and conversely, the slower a paint dries, the more it withstands hard wear and drastic weather conditions.

HOUSE PAINTS

Thus, a paint mixed largely with linseed oil as a medium, which scarcely begins to set in 24 or 36 hours, is used for outside house painting and sign-boards. When practical, two, three, or four weeks are allowed between coats of linseed oil paint, as the longer air has a chance to act upon the oil (oxidize it) the increasingly harder does paint become.

FURNITURE PAINT — INSIDE FLAT PAINTS

For furniture used indoors, varnish coats provide durability when applied over fast-drying finish paints, which can be more rapidly applied than linseed oil house paints. Also, many decorative effects placed upon a painted background are dependent upon complete hardness or dryness of the lower painted surface. For these reasons, "inside" paints (not exposed to the weather) are made with little or no linseed oil, but with turpentine, driers, etc., resulting in a "flat" surface, one that is soft and dry, but chalky, and therefore subject to being easily marred until varnished. We use inside flat white paint as a base for all light colors, toning them either with artists' oil colors or with japan tube paints to the desired color (always allowing for varnish and antiquing overtones to darken the final effect). Medium color backgrounds are generally japan tube colors mixed with turpentine and gold size or varnish to give a little more body. Black backgrounds are generally executed in flat black paint, bought in cans already mixed. *Background paints require at least twenty-four hours between coats.* We cannot emphasize this too strongly, for while a flat paint may appear to be dry in less time, it will soften up under a new application of paint, leaving a sur-face that is ridgy and far from smooth.

NO MODERN ENAMELS, LACQUERS OR FOUR-HOUR PAINTS

We purposely make no mention of these modern paints which were unknown to our old-time decorators, and which do not lend themselves to the processes we shall hereinafter describe.

JAPAN COLORS

Japan colors are equivalent to the old-time coach painters' colors, and are ideal for background paints. They contain dry color of various hues, combined with white lead (to make the paint opaque and cover the background), the whole ground well in a mixture of japan dryer, an oil preparation which aids in setting and drying the paint. Japan dryer may be bought separately and added to any paint wherein one desires a faster drying period. Japan colors may be bought in pound cans or in small tubes. For our purposes, we have adopted the small tubes, in spite of the proportionately higher cost, because tubes greatly facilitate taking out a small quantity and do not leave behind an air space to dry and harden the remaining paint. Japan paints in pound cans coat over with a hard surface every time they are exposed to a small air space, and this coating must be removed to the last tiny particle. Japan colors are often added to flat white paint when a light tinted background is desired.

Japan colors in tubes are also used for parts of our decorative designs, and for striping furniture in colors. There is no objection to combining japan colors with artists' oil colors either in mixing a background or in painting designs. In obtaining certain color tones, or certain degrees of opaqueness or transparency, the combining of artists' oil and japan colors is often quite necessary. Japan colors we use in this work are: Dark red, vermilion, chrome yellow light, chrome yellow medium, new green, coach green, azure blue, lamp black.

ARTISTS' OIL COLORS

Artists' oil colors are used for three general purposes. First: Their primary quality is a greater or less degree of transparency of color when used as an overtone with varnish or japan gold size. (Caution: If mixed only with turpentine, artists' oil colors do not "set" hard and fast, but under such conditions may be picked up by the brush and annoyingly "moved" when varnish or sizing is used over them.) The transparent colors of alizarin crimson, gamboge or yellow lake, Prussian blue, verdigris and mauve comprise the pigments that are transparent *in their own nature,* and as such are used for the floating over-glazes found on many flowers, and on parts of bronze stenciling. Artists' oil colors of raw umber, burnt umber, and burnt sienna are also partially transparent and are used in varying combinations to make a brown varnish overtone or "antique" finish. Raw umber and burnt umber are commonly used to produce the mellow overtone which most nearly resembles age. We have had to abandon Van Dyke brown because of its tendency to darken with age.

Second: They are used alone or in combination with japan paints to execute decorative designs.

Third: They are also used as before stated to vary the color of paints used for backgrounds.

The only exception to these three general statements is our use of white and black ground in oil, neither of which colors, in themselves, partake of transparency. White in oil is desirable because a tube of japan white has so much "body" that it sets hard in the tube and is difficult to dissolve when necessary. Phillips white is preferable to zinc or lead white, either of which may turn dark or leaden when combined with Prussian blue. Black in oil (ivory black, drop black, lamp black, etc.) is desirable, as it makes a smooth-flowing striping color, and does not dry so fast as to upset certain freehand bronze designs we occasionally wish to execute.

Artists' oil colors in tubes are seldom used alone on wood backgrounds unless a two-toned grained effect is desired. They contain no lead body to make them obscure the foundation wood or metal. They are, however, often used as *transparent* backgrounds against shining metal, such as new tin.

ASPHALTUM

Asphaltum, or asphaltum varnish, is a solution of mineral asphalt in varnish which produces a shiny, brownish-black effect, partially transparent in quality. It was usually employed upon tin trays, boxes, etc., and was frequently "fired" in baking ovens. Two or three coats were required to make a background that appeared opaque and almost black. When diluted with varnish, varying tones of golden brown are produced over bright tin.

According to chemists, asphaltum is a material that never completely dries, and for this reason is said to "bleed." Its tendency to soften slightly under body warmth makes it a general nuisance in the application of gold-leaf patterns. It also has the annoying quality of being easily scratched by such materials as sandpaper, and in retaining these scratch marks through all subsequent coats of varnish. Let the decorator who has a badly crackled scalloped-edge or lace-edge tray to restore beware of using sandpaper on the old finish until a new finish of several varnish coats has been built up for protection from scratches.

Asphaltum also requires that no fast-drying finish be used over it, as a crackled surface is sure to result. A twenty-four-hour varnish or slower must be used.

TURPENTINE

Turpentine is a volatile vegetable medium, mixed with pigments to form a background surface. It eventually evaporates, leaving a dull surface and the pigments in a rather chalky condition. In our work, it is better to mix a little varnish, gold size, or linseed oil with the turpentine and pigment to form a harder surface. Over absolutely new wood it is best to use as first coat, a paint mixed largely with turpentine, since it penetrates more deeply into the wood.

Turpentine is never used with paints in the execution of a design upon a painted background. It is never used in mixing a striping color. These two prohibitions we cannot stress too strongly, as they are the most common errors of the amateur decorator.

RAW LINSEED OIL

Raw linseed oil is a light-colored vegetable oil and is used on wood surfaces where slow drying or long wearing qualities are desired. As before stated, it makes a paint that withstands weather conditions, if given plenty of time to oxidize between coats. It may be used in varnish to slow up the drying time, and to make the varnish finish more enduring. Raw linseed oil may be applied with a fine drawing pen either to a flat paint surface or a dry glossy surface, set aside for at least four or five days and then be given an overlay of gold leaf or colored bronze powders.

BOILED LINSEED OIL

"Boiled" linseed oil is a raw linseed to which a small amount of dryer has been added to speed up its drying time. It may be used largely as raw linseed oil is used, providing it is understood that because of faster drying its lifetime is proportionately lessened. It is more brownish in color than raw linseed oil but not so transparent.

CRUDE OIL

Crude oil, a dark brown, molasses-colored mineral oil, is used with pumice and a soft cloth in the final rubbing down of a glossy finish. Afterwards a clean soft cloth is used to collect all traces of pumice and oil, and achieve the final polishing.

Marbleized paneling, with cream-white scroll running between. Found in the Warner House, Portsmouth, N. H., when a break-front bookcase was moved. This painting probably done about 1758 when new owners were preparing the house for a daughter's wedding.

Panels of rose-pink graining, framed with a gray-green marbling, at Cogswell's Grant, formerly a part of Ipswich, Mass. The two panels over the fireplace are original, having been successfully uncovered. Courtesy of Mr. and Mrs. Bertram K. Little.

PUMICE

Pumice is a finely-ground stone dust used with crude oil, as just stated, in the dull finishing of antique pieces. We purchase pumice at drug stores because it seems more finely pulverized than that securable at hardware stores. Pumice may also be used with water and the palm of the hand to remove imperfections in finish before the final coat or coats of varnish. The same results may be secured by using #00 sandpaper, or #0 steel wool, care being taken to remove all bits of sand dust and all particles of steel wool before varnishing.

ALCOHOL

Denatured alcohol dissolves shellac, and we use it chiefly as a cleaning fluid on old trays and furniture to which damaged coats of shellac still cling. Contrary to our custom today, varnishes were seldom used as an original finish, but an alcohol-solvent gum surface like shellac was given them. In course of time this old surface has turned white from moisture, or dark from impurities and accumulations of dirt. So a judicious cleaning with a soft cloth and alcohol is tried before restoring any missing parts of design. Alcohol is also a slow paint solvent, and may be used to gradually dissolve overcoats of modern paint in uncovering an original design. Caution is here given concerning the use of alcohol cleaning on "country tin" as made in America, since little or no finish appears over these painted designs and the decoration may be irreparably damaged when touched with alcohol. It is a wise decorator who knows when to use alcohol as a cleaner and when to leave it strictly alone.

Alcohol can also be employed to dilute shellac, the common furniture finish used in modern factories. Having no fondness for shellac when more enduring varnishes are available, we put shellac way back on our paint shelves and leave it distinctly alone, with the one exception stated below.

SHELLAC

Our only use for shellac may be to correct a coat of paint or varnish that did not dry completely, and one coat of shellac may dry out the remaining stickiness. Shellac, however, should never be the *last* coat applied to a piece.

VARNISH

Varnish is composed of various vegetable gums, oils and dryers, and appears on the market in many varieties today. We select a high-grade twenty-four-hour varnish for our purpose, remembering that it must be applied in a room heated to at least 70 degrees and on a non-humid, fair-weather day. There is in varnish a volatile oil which *must* evaporate within the first few hours of its application, otherwise it is imprisoned, and the varnish surface is left gummy. In cases of emergency, or in bad weather, a four-hour varnish may be used, providing we are not expecting to stencil or do any other extensive stunts with it while it is drying.

Varnish is one of the most versatile of our painting materials. As before stated, a little of it is mixed with japan colors in forming a background paint on furniture. When paint is used on non-absorbent metal grounds it is always well to use varnish in its composition that it may cling to the slippery metal surface. Varnish is used with many pigments in flowing on a decorative design. It is used to mix all striping colors. It is used in the laying of gold leaf when a slow medium is desired. Finally it is used with mellow transparent colors to simulate age, as a protective finish upon most of these old-time painted pieces, adding to the endurance of our craftsmanship.

Japan Gold Size

As its name implies, japan gold size was originally designed for the application of gold-leaf patterns. Under various trade names and in the hands of many different manufacturers it is a highly variable product. Some brands dry in fifteen minutes, some in four hours and others may range between. It is necessary to experiment personally with a brand until we learn its drying speed and then proceed accordingly. The slow type, which takes about four hours to dry, may in bad weather become the equivalent of varnish (since varnish must not be used on a bad weather day) and extend its drying time to twenty hours. A very fast japan gold size may be slowed down by the admixture of twenty-four-hour varnish. Here again experiment must teach us as to the proportion of each ingredient. A few drops of raw linseed oil in japan gold size may also produce a desirable drying speed. We use japan gold size for the flowing on of many decorative patterns in color where smoothness of paint is not sacrificed by its fast-setting proclivities. A little japan gold size may be used instead of varnish in the mixing of japan colors as a background paint. When a gold-leaf pattern is to be laid, we mix a little gold bronze powder with the japan gold size in order that the design may be easily visible. Our favorite "japan gold size" is a mixture of Hiburnish bronzing liquid and twenty-four-hour varnish, half and half.

Gum Arabic

A solution of gum arabic, sugar syrup and water (or wine) is used to apply a fine-line design with a crow quill pen upon a flat paint background. In recording such a design upon traceolene, gum arabic *must* be used instead of raw linseed oil as previously described, because the oil spreads hopelessly over the tracing paper surface. Gum arabic lines so penned are allowed to dry and are subsequently breathed upon to revive slight adhesive qualities before applying gold leaf or bronze powder. Beware of using such a method over a glossy or varnish surface, for two reasons: One, the gum arabic lines may "skid" from their position; second, breathing upon the gum arabic design may revive latent stickiness in the glossy background and so spoil the clarity of our pattern. Caution is also given that this gum arabic solution is very sensitive to humid weather conditions; and if used on such a day, plenty of time for drying should be allowed; and the breathing upon it should be omitted completely, as there is already enough moisture imprisoned in it from the humidity.

Paint and Varnish Remover

As its name implies, paint and varnish remover is used to soften paints and varnishes and facilitate their removal. On soft wood pieces, it is dangerous for a novice to use a steel scraper in conjunction with paint remover, as there is grave likelihood of digging into the wood. Steel wool plus paint remover is far safer. Paint remover is employed in softening up small brushes used for painted designs, such brushes *having* to be perfectly flexible before using. This applies particularly to striping brushes. Caution is hereby given that larger brushes, such as those used for varnish and background paints, must *under no conditions* be placed in paint remover. Small particles of wax floating in the remover will ruin large brushes for further usefulness. These wax particles are placed in remover for the purpose of holding the partially dissolved paints in suspension preparatory to removal. Paint remover thoroughly chilled to solidify wax particles may be strained through several thicknesses of cheesecloth and set aside for the cleaning of stencils.

Tincture of Benzoin

Tincture of benzoin may be used to thin down a mixture of sizing or varnish which has been exposed to the air so long that it has started to solidify in globules. The addition of a few drops of benzoin will cause these globules to break down and become fluid again. This is entirely an emergency measure when painting a design, and is not used in a large quantity of varnish or sizing that has become stringy from exposure to air. Tincture of benzoin on a soft cloth may be quickly rubbed over a white cloudy ring where varnish or old shellac has been subjected to moisture. The benzoin seems to revive the old finish to its former clear and transparent state.

Carbona

Carbona, carbon tetrachloride or other rapidly evaporating cleansing fluid, is used to correct any mistakes that may be made in painting decorative designs. It is well to make all corrections immediately, as the longer a paint stands the harder it is to dissolve and wipe away. Thus, if harder wiping becomes necessary, the background paint surface is more easily injured.

Gold Leaf

Gold leaf may be obtained from manufacturers in a number of different shades depending upon the metals with which it is alloyed. For our purposes two colors chiefly are employed: One known as rich gold, full orange gold in coloring, which comes mounted upon a small sheet of tissue paper to facilitate handling; and the other, a pale lemon gold which is almost silvery in tone, a color often found upon old-time patterns. Pale (lemon) gold does not come mounted on tissue unless specifically ordered, but may be lifted by laying a square of wax paper upon it carefully. Warmth of the hand against the wax paper causes the gold leaf to adhere to the wax surfaces. In this way it may be transferred to the pattern as desired. Gold leaf which remains upon the wax paper over night or longer may become so incorporated with it as to resist transference to the sized pattern.

Silver Leaf

Silver leaf comes in slightly larger sheets than gold leaf, unmounted upon tissue. It may be handled with wax paper as above described. Silver leaf is used chiefly in preparing backgrounds on lace-edge trays, as will be subsequently described. It was also used as a background for certain color designs. Occasionally designs similar to gold-leaf patterns were laid in silver leaf and varnished over with a gold-colored varnish to simulate gold. A very detrimental quality is inherent in silver leaf, since it is subject to tarnish even when under a number of varnish coats. In some designs this adds to the appearance of age, but in others it detracts from the ultimate effect. There is no known deterrent to this tarnish habit.

Aluminum Leaf

Aluminum leaf is equivalent to silver leaf and is not subject to tarnish. The ancients also had a thin tinfoil which they used under a golden-colored varnish to represent gold leaf.

Bronze Powders

Bronzes, in decorators' parlance, are pulverized metals in many colors, not just in bronze coloring. Those we commonly use are in silver color (called aluminum bronze), pale gold of a very finely ground composition, rich orange gold, copper brown, matt green and brilliant fire. These powders are sold by the ounce or pound, an ounce being sufficient to stencil with for a year or more.

For practical purposes we move the bronze powders from their ounce envelopes into a stoppered bottle from which small quantities may be shaken out as desired. When using the powders we find that a strip of heavy velour about six inches wide is very advantageous. Small quantities of bronzes are ranged up and down the midrib of this velour, starting with silver and graduating in tone to the brilliant fire bronze. From this velour carpet a few grains of bronze may be picked up on a piece of velvet and applied to our pattern. When finished, the velour strip is folded over on its midrib, rolled up and put away in the paint basket.

Velvet

Pieces of old-time *pure silk-back* velvet should be found in grandmother's attic for use in stenciling. Modern transparent velvet is prohibited. Cotton-back velvets or velveteens are equally useless. Tiny particles of thread come out of these velvets and imbed themselves in varnish where we least want them. But modern pure silk velvet may be purchased in the dress goods department, if old scraps cannot be found. These pieces are hemmed on two sides so that no raw edges are exposed, then seamed like a cuff, because raveling edges leave bits of thread in our stencil work.

Higgins Waterproof Drawing Ink

Waterproof black drawing ink is occasionally used to do fine black lines upon gold-leaf work.

Crow Quill Pen

A crow quill pen is a very fine steel drawing pen used with waterproof ink in fine-line drawing upon gold leaf, etc. This pen is also used with raw linseed oil, as stated previously, or with gum arabic, in applying a fine pattern in gold leaf or colored bronzes.

ETCHING TOOL

Any strong fine-pointed tool, such as a cuticle knife or fine steel knitting needle, may be used to etch gold leaf. Occasionally a bundle of three or four needles should be fashioned into an etching tool where many fine parallel lines are found in the old etching.

BRUSHES

Brushes are of several kinds. First, soft-bristle varnish brushes, ranging from one-half inch (for small work) to two inches in width, used for all background painting and varnishing; second, very soft hair (camel's hair, sable, etc.) brushes, used for our decorative design work, *with square tips* varying in width from one-quarter inch down to the finest hair pencils. Since the professional decorator generally aims for perfect smoothness, he does *not* use a stiff bristle brush as artists do on canvas. Background paint and varnish brushes are kept flexible between usings by submerging the bristles completely in raw linseed oil.

It is very necessary to learn what size brush is proper to use for each particular problem. Thus when painting design units that are an inch or more in width we use a square-tipped (show-card painter's) brush with hairs from three-fourths of an inch to one inch in length, and at least one-quarter of an inch wide. A small brush used for this purpose is not only inefficient but is apt to allow uneven drying. For smaller design work we use the smallest quill brushes, with hairs three-fourths of an inch long, varying in thickness according to the delicacy of our lines. These quill brushes are mounted by soft solder on small handles shaved to fit, and are thinned down into graduating sizes. Trimming is done by cutting away outside hairs at the base only. Fine hairline brushes may have only a few hairs, but each must be of equal length. Constant inspection of design brushes for short hairs is imperative. This we do by taking hold of the hair tips and turning them backward toward the base. If any short hairs stick out at the side, they are immediately removed, for perfect brush strokes require that short hairs do not escape from our control when rounding outward or convex curves. Striping brushes are made of one-and-one-half-inch hairs set in a small quill which we do *not* equip with a wooden handle as we do the design brushes. A striper is also carefully trimmed to varying thicknesses depending upon the width of stripe desired. All thinned or short hairs are cut at the base of quill *only*.

We have chosen the foregoing specified lengths after experimenting with many sizes of brushes. With a shorter brush we sacrifice in flow of paint and sweep of line, while with a longer brush we have difficulty in keeping perfect control from tip to base.

Traceolene

Traceolene, used for recording old designs, is a very fine tracing paper through which the most obscure patterns are visible. It is fragile and must be handled gently after the patterns are traced upon it. For reproducing a stencil pattern, the design units are first traced on traceolene by a fine pen, and then retraced on tracing linen before cutting. Traceolene may also be painted with colors and gold sizing or varnish, in which case it is laid upon the patterns, and the basic parts of the record are made directly over the original. After all details are filled in, just as noted on the old example, the traceolene pattern may be mounted, preferably upon a piece of stiff paper painted the background color of the original. Scotch adhesive tape is used to mount the pattern on its background. For perfect keeping in a file, wax paper should be placed over these painted patterns.

Tracing Linen for Stencils

Tracing linen, used for stencils, is a drawing linen treated with a starch sizing for transparency. There are many qualities, but the imported English linen for architectural use is most transparent. It seems like paper, and is the toughest kind of material of its thickness we know. Stencils cut in this material must be executed with fine-pointed embroidery scissors, since a knife cutting across the threads is apt to stretch and ruffle them. Used stencils are cleaned with carbona or paint remover *on both sides* and wiped dry before putting away in folders.

Transfer Paper

Transfer paper, to be used instead of greasy commercial carbon paper, may be made by rubbing a block of magnesium on the back of a sheet of ordinary tracing paper (not traceolene). Unused lines may later be wiped off with a damp cloth.

Scissors for Stencil Cutting

Scissors, for cutting stencils, must be very fine pointed and kept well sharpened. Manicure scissors are not desirable, as the curved points frequently interfere with the direction of the stencil to be cut. Straight-pointed scissors are requisite for cutting straight lines, and can be made to cut curved lines with ease. So we select fine quality embroidery or surgical scissors with points that cut *immediately* upon puncturing the paper.

Small Bottle Caps

Cups used to hold small quantities of gold sizing or varnish while we are painting decorative designs may be salvaged from many bottles in the medicine cabinet or kitchen. We always remove any cork or cardboard filler that the caps may be padded with. Flatter and wider screw top covers, such as those on cold cream jars, are useful when mixing striping colors, since the one-and-one-half-inch striping brush may then be laid its entire length in the striping mixture.

Ruler or Metal Tape Measure

A long ruler or metal tape measure is used for accuracy in centering our designs.

Basket for Materials

A basket similar to a two-handled market basket with the top removed has proven convenient for handy access to our decorative paint materials. Ranged along the bottom of our basket are our tube colors, the japan colors separated from the artists' oil colors. Against one long side we place our ruler, or metal tape measure, and long-handled show-card brushes. In order that these materials may be easily accessible we make strips of small pockets out of heavy material and tack them to the top edge of our paint basket. Into these pockets go our bottles of bronze powders, our velour strip with bronzes ready to use, our pieces of stencil velvet, our gold and silver leaf, bottle of tincture of benzoin, carbona, paint remover, bottle of japan gold size, gum arabic, raw linseed oil, Higgins waterproof ink and stencil scissors. Our tiny design brushes, drawing pen and etching tool are kept in a flat tin cigarette box placed on top of the tube colors in the bottom of our basket. With this equipment we may paint most patterns in our repertoire. Larger containers of alcohol, varnish, etc., are kept near at hand on the studio closet shelf.

PART TWO

The Methods for Applying Decorative Designs

The Methods for Applying Decorative Designs

BRONZE stenciling is one of the simplest methods employed by our old-time decorators, though it is by no means among the earliest. In fact, it is quite the opposite. Early methods of decorating, such as were used by the japanners of about 1720, are so highly complex that they will not serve the purpose of introducing the new student to our art by easy stages. Thus we propose to take up our subject of decorative paint methods in a more or less reverse chronological order, since nineteenth century decline in art reduced everything to its quickest and simplest form, for speedy quantity production.

STENCILING IN BRONZE

So let us begin with bronze stenciling — the technique used upon most Boston rockers, Hitchcock-type chairs and wood-seat Windsors dating from 1820 to 1850 and later. Bronze stenciling was also used upon hundreds of trays, spice boxes, trinket boxes and a thousand and one articles of tinware too numerous to mention. Let us follow stenciling backwards through greater elaboration to its early beginnings on metal trays that were probably imported from England, France or the Orient. For it is my belief that bronze stenciling came into being through the cunning of Oriental craftsmen, whose lacquer work made them past masters in handling decorative metal powders.

In modern parlance, stenciling is a method of applying paint by means of a square-ended scrub or brush, through holes cut in a piece of stiff paper, oiled cardboard or sheet metal, called a stencil. But outside of the *name* stenciling, we can find little similarity between this modern process and the antique bronze work of our early craftsmen. In the old days, the decorator first cut a "theorem" or stencil in copybook paper by means of a fine-pointed knife. This paper was placed upon sheet metal or glass before cutting, to keep the paper edge from turning downwards. Next — but let us turn to an old-time decorator's guide book for unquestioned authority on this so-called "forgotten art":

"The ground for this work must be varnished with a mixture of copal varnish, with an equal quantity of old linseed oil; and whatever figures are to be formed in bronzing must be represented by holes cut through pieces of paper. Lay these patterns on the work, when the varnish is so dry as to be but slightly adhesive, but not press them down any more than is requisite to keep the paper in place. Then take a piece of soft glove leather, moisten it in some dry bronze, and apply it to the figures, beginning at the edges; tap the figure gently with the leather, and the bronze will stick to the varnish according to the pattern. Thus any figure may be produced in a variety of shades, by applying the bronze more freely to some parts of the work than to other. If some internal parts of the figures require to be more distinct than others they may be wrought by their peculiar patterns, or may be edged with dark colored paint. In some work it may be well to extend the varnish no farther than the intended figures, in which case, any projecting or branching parts of the figures, may be drawn with a camel-hair pencil, and the patterns may in some measure be suspended with.[1] In either case the work must afterwards have one or more coats of copal or shellac varnish."[2]

MATERIALS FOR TRACING

For our present day purposes we replace the copybook paper stencil with architects' tracing linen, a tough and semi-transparent material. Its thinness is ideal, and its partial transparency often gives us an opportunity to trace an old design directly upon it. When labor is now so costly, we feel more justified in making stencils of a material primarily designed to withstand severe usage. Caution is hereby given to protect tracing linen from all forms of moisture, which affects the starch sizing with wrinkles and distortions. Such damaged linen is useless for our purposes, as it has lost its transparency, its stiffness and its keen flat edge necessary to control the stenciling bronze powders. Tracing linen can stand oils, carbona, and even paint remover, but it cannot survive one drop of moisture.

Occasionally an old stencil pattern which we wish to reproduce is too indistinct to be seen through the translucent texture of tracing linen. So a first tracing is made on traceolene (a *very* transparent but fragile tracing paper recently put on the market) and is retraced again with fine drawing pen and waterproof ink upon the tracing linen. Great attention MUST be paid to all the tiny curves and quirks in the original pattern, for by these

[1]This suggests the method we call freehand bronze.   See Examples on pages 211, 216 and black rose.
[2]From a book copyrighted in 1825, and already in its fifth edition in 1826, published at Concord, N. H., called "A Select Collection of Valuable and Curious Arts" by Rufus Porter.

infinitesimal accuracies is a stencil given distinction. If traceolene is not available, we can outline the original stencil pattern with white paint and a little sizing so that it becomes visible directly through the linen, and may be forthwith traced thereon. Immediately after tracing, our white paint may be removed from the original pattern surface by wiping it with a turpentine moistened cloth.

CUTTING OF STENCILS

We modern decorators cut our tracing linen stencils with straight-bladed, sharp-pointed embroidery or surgical scissors, specially selected for our job. The student may wonder why the whole of our stencil cutting is not done with a sharp-pointed razor blade. The answer is that pulling a razor blade against the threads of our tracing linen allows the threads to stretch and the edge to ruffle. If we used paper, as the old-timers did, then we might adopt either a well-sharpened knife or a razor for cutting. We have seen many old-time stencils, however, so fragile now that even museum officials hesitate to handle them. So we gamble on the greater wearing qualities of tracing linen, hoping that time will not cause our stencils to become brittle.

Cutting of stencils at first seems very difficult. It is well to start with large simple designs and progress to those with tinier detail. Fine curving lines such as flower stems and tiny leaves may be "started" by piercing with the point of a razor blade. Experience will teach the stencil cutter how certain curves bending from right to left cut easier on the outside of the curve where scissor blades do not press hard against the edge of the tracing linen. (This sentence may not seem understandable to the reader, but the problem will present itself when stencil cutting is actually undertaken.) Pressing against the linen edge with the broadside of our scissors will often tear the stencil. So in order to cut the outside of a curve counter-clockwise (for a right-handed person) from right to left, we often reverse the linen and cut from the back side. A fine S-curve line is started at the center and cut outward to one end of the letter loop, then retraced to the center and cut the other half length, doubling back to the center for completion. Every line — no matter how fine — is made with two parallel scissor cuts. In cutting a small area, or leaf unit, care is taken to puncture the paper near the center of the space, in order that the edge, as desired, may be clean cut. Hardest of all, is the cutting of tiny dots, which must be done by cutting around with scissor tips in a tiny circle. A punch always seems to be the wrong size, and is inclined to leave ragged edges.

VARNISH FOR STENCILING

Now when the stencils required are all cut, and the article to be stenciled is already prepared with its proper background — twenty-four hours or more dry — we give the background a thin, evenly-spread coat of twenty-four-hour varnish. This is allowed to dry from one to two, three, or four hours, depending upon the drying quality of the weather, until it is almost "set" — which stage is decided by testing with the finger. Practice will teach the decorator to recognize this ideal stage for stenciling, when the varnish gives notice to the finger that a slight stickiness is still present but allows the finger to come away clean. Varnish, we learn, is in an oily state when first exposed to the air. Then the volatile oil starts evaporating into the atmosphere, allowing the varnish to approach what is a highly gummy stage. Last of all, this gummy consistency changes to an almost dry state, which is when we capture it for stenciling. The varnish stays in this stage for about an hour, so the decorator must learn to work fast if she wishes to complete the stenciling in this length of time. Should the varnish become too dry after stencil work is partly executed, the best procedure is to revarnish twenty-four hours or more *later,* and continue with stenciling as before. Do not attempt to revarnish on the same day, or the stenciled bronze will be picked up and "moved" by the varnish brush.

The decorator who wishes to have more time in executing the stenciling may slow up the varnish setting by the addition of turpentine or linseed oil as the original recipe directed. This will delay the varnish drying an unpredictable length of time, and requires that the decorator be willing to accept the time for stenciling whenever the varnish arrives at the right stage. We have known linseed oil and varnish, mixed one-fifth oil to four-fifths varnish, to take between two and three days to arrive at the desired stage, but then all day long the stenciling was possible. And we might add, the smooth shining beauty of this stenciling was a joy to behold. In finishing those particular stenciled chairs we were careful to use a varnish finish of the same mixture, since a faster drying finish might have crackled the surface. (Any shellac used on top of this oil-and-varnish stenciling would have been fatal.)

In bad weather, we must not use a twenty-four-hour varnish, since the volatile oil does not evaporate properly in a humid or moisture-ladened atmosphere. If we *must* stencil then, there are several substitutes we may use for the twenty-four-hour varnish. We may use Super Valspar, which sets in about four hours in good weather, but becomes more nearly the equivalent of a twenty-four-hour varnish applied under ideal atmospheric conditions. Or we may substitute a four-hour japan gold size, which would be far too fast for us in fine weather. Still further, we may concoct a fast-drying mixture of speedy japan gold size, and our twenty-four-hour varnish, if the brand of sizing we have at hand happens to be faster than the four-hour variety. In any case, the article is set aside to await the required state of near-dryness we require.

APPLICATION OF BRONZE POWDER

With the proper moment for stenciling at last arrived, we place the surface to be ornamented in a horizontal position (if possible) and lay the stencil in place, where it slightly adheres to the varnish (or sizing). If stenciling is attempted in an upright or vertical position there is grave danger of having the bronze powder slip down behind the stencil where it is not desired. Next we take a piece of old-time, silk-back velvet and wrap it around our index finger on the right hand (if we are right-handed), holding all ends of the velvet firmly hidden in the palm of our hand. With this "velvet finger" we transfer a few grains of bronze powder from the velour strip in which it is kept, to the stencil pattern, employing for this process a horizontal polishing motion, and continuing until the section has become as brightly laden with bronze powder as we desire.

The motion used in applying bronze powders to a stencil is most important. The novice is inclined to dab *at* the stencil with an up-and-down motion which allows the tracing linen to jump slightly, and bronze powder to fly under our stencil edge. We must learn to keep our velvet finger on the stencil and varnish surface, and polish with a rapid oscillating motion as if we were cleaning silver. We must do this polishing very lightly, for pressure will scar the varnish surface. Pressure while stenciling will also pull threads out of the velvet and imbed them in the varnish. Such a misadventure is hardly noticeable until our colored overtones are laid on later; then we begin to discover a dirty, rough surface on our stencil work. Should such a condition appear, it is best to build up two or three coats of heavy clear varnish (to protect our design work) and then sandpaper lightly. The threads that are then above the varnish surface will be clipped off by friction and we will have no further trouble with them. Sandpapering before the varnish protection is applied would go right through our stenciled pattern, and require that we re-stencil.

It is difficult to describe what proportion of the stencil is filled in with the velvet and bronze application. In very tiny units, of course, we cannot make the design register unless practically all the stencil is well filled with bronze powder (see example, page 179). In large open units, such as a peach, we high-light the center by a circular motion, and the edges are given a faint definition by rubbing all around from the outside edge of the stencil inward toward the open center of the stencil. All jagged leaves require that the velvet stroke be mostly from outside the leaf points inward toward the open center of the stencil — where the bronze is usually allowed to thin out to nothingness, according to the decorator's wish. A sudden shift from bright bronze shading to darkness is not desirable; the bronze must be carefully graded down from brilliance to total disappearance. Only by this means does the shaded unit look attractive, and convincingly real.

The varnished surface which lies directly beneath the holes in the stencil we imagine to be like the pores of our skin. When thoroughly filled with grains of bronze, the pattern is as bright as we can make it; when very scantily filled, the pattern is considered to be in shadow. Care is taken to fill the "pores" gradually, just faintly at first, but polishing in with more and more grains as desired. We always keep in mind the fact that more grains of bronze may be easily added, but they may not be removed without great difficulty.

WHY VELVET?

It will be noticed that we have discarded the instruction to stencil with soft glove leather as originally described in the 1825 book. We have experimented with chamois and soft finish leathers, but have not obtained as favorable results as with the velvet we have adopted. Besides, at least two old-time decorators are known to have used velvet nubbins — i. e., a piece of velvet in which a wad of cotton was tied to make a knob the size of a finger tip. Mr. George Lord, of Portland, stenciled this way; and Mr. Willard Brooks of Hancock, New Hampshire, whose kit was found under the eaves of his home several years ago, had a similar velvet wad in his outfit. But gradation of bronze from strong high light to a subtle disappearance cannot be easily

Stencil Kit used by Z. Willard Brooks, a decorator and gilder of Hancock, N. H. Found under the eaves of his house. Courtesy of Mr. Maro S. Brooks, Hancock, N. H.

achieved with a wadded applicator. These two old-time decorators both experienced difficulty in making their bronzes disappear smoothly into darkness. Subsequent to 1835, however (when most of their decorating was done), speedy factory production was already causing a demand for *non-composed* stencil patterns, wherein careful shading was not a primary requisite. Late stenciling, built for an all-in-one application, generally used smaller leaf and flower motifs quite careless in form. The velvet nubbin would do that sort of stencil work satisfactorily. Still later stencilers appear to have used — of all things! — bronze paint mixed with some liquid and applied with a brush, if we are able to judge by appearances. We, however, have set our heart upon reproducing the *most beautiful* examples of bronze stenciling, and have found success only with the velvet-wrapped finger herewith described.

BRONZES TO BE WELL UNDER CONTROL

There are a number of cautions to be observed if fine stenciling is to be achieved. First of all, every grain of bronze powder used must be incorporated in the varnish pores. There must be no allowing of unadhered bronze to stand upon the surface of our design when the stencil is picked up. There must be no "free" bronze balancing upon the edge of a stencil, ready to fly out of place onto our background at the lifting of our linen paper patterns. Stencils should be carefully cleaned on *both* sides with paint remover before being put away, or cleaned oftener if they seem to require it. From the front, stray bits of bronze powder need to be removed, and from the back, small particles of varnish that might harden and thicken the stencil edge. Good bronze stenciling requires a thin edge and perfect smoothness between stencil and background. If, in some part of a design, the stencil is to be completely reversed, be *sure* the stencil is perfectly cleaned on both sides before reversing. Nothing is more annoying than a few stray specks of bronze dotting an otherwise perfect background, the result of failure to clean the stencil. Mend breaks in a stencil with Scotch adhesive tape, *on top*.

DISSECTING A COMPOSED PATTERN INTO UNITS

While late style stenciled chairs and tinware were ornamented with designs cut all in one piece, we find the better patterns were executed with composite stencils. We must learn to dissect a design by observing where two units touch, and where one seems to pass behind the other into mysterious depths. In general, the composition begins with the center foreground, against which the adjacent sections are stenciled and so on until the outside edges of the problem are reached. Thus in stenciling a Hitchcock chair pattern, the bowl or basket is placed first, filled with the central flower (or fruit), the ones to the right and left next, and then whatever units flank the bowl and contents just defined. On stenciled landscape trays, the process becomes quite complex, but may be figured out along these same lines.

OVER-STENCILING

Getting down to specific cases, there are a few stunts peculiar to bronze stenciling. It is possible to stencil in detail sections such as the seeds on a strawberry, and shade on an over-stenciling directly on top without losing the previous details. But this requires that *all* open varnish pores under the detailed stencil spaces be *completely* filled with bronze powder before overlaying the next stencil. If they are so filled, the second stenciling does not "take" in these spots. It is also possible, by the same means, to place a glowing cloud about a rose center, if desired.

SHADING OF VEINS

Another stunt is the shading of leaves by a method which we call modeling, or high-lighting. This is not to be confused with leaves that are veined with a separate fine-line stencil in bright bronzes. Our high-light veins are applied to leaves that have been stenciled purposely with bright tips but dark centers. Into this shadow a midrib is faintly placed by laying a curved-edge stencil or "theorem," and lightly brushing over this curve with our velvet finger and bronze powder. Next, subsidiary veins are added to right and left with the same curved edge until the leaf stands out as if modeled after Nature. Such perfect detailing of leaves is far more difficult to do than the previously mentioned fine-line veining, and is generally found in stenciling prior to 1830.

THE SILHOUETTE STENCIL

Another stunt found principally upon tin trays is the reverse stencil, or silhouette form. Here the pattern appears in black against a smooth or clouded bronze background. It is often found in the curved corners of rectangular trays, as it adjusts itself to the two-way curve better than a straight stencil. In cutting these stencils of lacy silhouettes it is best to cut all the center or stencil holes first, leaving the edge trimming until last; otherwise, the tiny pattern will be difficult to handle. In stenciling at a curved corner we have our hardest problem, since the entire stencil may not conform to the double complexity of curves at this point. So the silhouette form is laid down and stenciled through the center, then the two ends of the stencil are done alternately, while allowing the opposite end to remain free of the varnished tray.

OVERTONES OF TRANSPARENT COLOR

Although several different shades of bronze powders were available to the old-time decorator, most bright colors were achieved by an overshading of transparent color, flowed on in varnish or sizing. Colors used for this work are alizarin crimson, yellow lake or gamboge, Prussian blue and verdigris, with raw umber or burnt umber to tone down their brilliance. Some trays appear to have been stenciled mostly in silver and pale gold, colored with blues, browns, and greens, as if to simulate the mother-of-pearl made popular by Queen Victoria.

STENCILING ON NATURAL WOOD

Once in a great while we find bronze stenciling ornamenting mahogany or rosewood pieces. Here two methods are used: Either the panel, post or other section to be stenciled is finished in ebony black, or else black paint is used directly behind the stencil units only, extending no farther than the outermost tips of the design. This latter method is suggested by a phrase in the directions for stenciling quoted near the beginning of this chapter. Rarest of all is stenciling to be found applied directly to mahogany or rosewood in natural wood finish.

STENCILING ON COLORS

Stenciling is occasionally applied against dark blue, dark green or vermilion backgrounds, but something is sacrificed in so doing. It seems that bronze stencils require a black background to be truly effective. We suppose that the illusion of disappearance into shadow is easily achieved where black (the color of darkness) is employed. But color backgrounds fail to lend this suggestion of shadow and so lessen the effectiveness of that shading which is the greatest attribute of bronze stenciling. On no account does a good decorator stencil on yellow, without putting black directly behind, or arranging for a black panel. Yellow, the color of light and sunshine, does not suggest any shadow whatsoever.

PRACTICE WORK

Now that the general idea of stenciling in bronzes has been definitely described, it is well for the beginner to start practicing the technique. We blacken unwrinkled wrapping paper, shelf paper, or newspapers with two coats of flat black, and varnish as if this painted paper were a tray or chair to be decorated. (Do not use unglazed cardboard, unless it is well prepared with shellac, to stop the porous surface.) Long practice may be required to achieve an understanding of how the bronze powders are kept under control. The common error is to stencil while the varnish is gummy and to use too many grains of bronze. If the powders are kept on a piece of heavy velour, as suggested in our chapter on materials, then the student will find that taking bronzes from the outer edge (away from the midrib) will be most successful, since the distribution here is ordinarily less dense. We shall study the different methods of shading peaches, and practice to make them look round and luscious. We shall observe how a bunch of grapes is built one by one, in graduating sizes. Let us practice the modeling of leaves with curving high lights, and see that the veins all grow naturally outward from the center vein. By observation we shall learn how the old-time decorators used silver, the brightest of bronzes, for the main or central units of importance, flanking them with leaves or other motifs in pale gold or orange gold. We do not jump directly from silver to orange gold, as the necessary transition of pale gold cannot be supplied by the imagination. Some fruits and flowers are composed of silver high lights with pale gold shading near the depths, which combination allows orange gold leaves to be used in juxtaposition. Fire-colored bronze is often found on stenciled strawberries. In short, let the decorator take old-time designs for his guide, as they have been ours in this study of painted decoration.

FREEHAND METHOD LOOKS SIMILAR

Now that we have explained the mysteries of old-time stenciling, do not make the mistake of thinking that everything in shaded gold is achieved with stencils. We must remember that there is a freehand bronze method which might easily be mistaken for stenciling, as indeed, the two processes are often found together in one and the same pattern. Our old-time decorators had a thorough understanding of *many* methods, and did not hesitate to use whatever combination best suited their problems.

ADDITION OF FREEHAND PAINTING

Then, too, frequent color details are used on stencil patterns to relieve the monotony of mechanical work. On landscape trays there are fuzzy trees in olive green paint, patted in with an almost dry brush, and bushes near the ground done by the same process. On some stencil border trays there are freehand brush strokes to add color or refined embellishment; on the *best* stencil chairs there are often freehand gold-leaf trimmings. So we must learn to view every pattern with an analytical mind, recognizing each process as it presents itself.

PART THREE

Brush-Stroke Painting

Brush-Stroke Painting

BRUSH-STROKE PAINTING covers primarily those designs and borders that are achieved by simple swings of a well-controlled brush. The color tone is generally flat, with little shading, and yet a highly decorative effect may be achieved. Many articles of household use or adornment were so decorated, varying from furniture and tinware to Bristol, Lowestoft, and other products of the potter's art. Country-made Windsor chairs often had simple brush-stroke leaf sprays, in flat color like striping, of which more will soon be said.

ON "COUNTRY" TIN

But by far the greatest number of articles found to be ornamented with brush-stroke patterns are those infinitely varied articles in tin, which were made by the country tinsmith. So much similarity of technique runs through many of these designs that it is our belief the apprentices were taught how to do this painting during their years of service. For unpainted tinplate was found to disintegrate when exposed to moisture, and to resist rust when given a heavy coat of paint or asphaltum, a process called by the time-honored name of "japanning" (indeed, after the 1750's this term japanning had come to mean *any* type of painted decoration).

ON FINE TEA TRAYS

As we go higher up the scale to elaborately "japanned tea trays and waiters," we can never quite get away from brush-stroke details, in minor parts of the designs. For those decorators who ascended to great heights were first and foremost complete masters of this simplest color technique. Unlike the modern designer who often applies color in blobs, the old-time decorator with his brush laid on his paints in perfection of *form* and *rhythm* down to the tiniest detail of leaf spray and curling tendril. Once the student gets thoroughly in mind the idea that she is *modeling* a flower in paint, and portraying its *true form* with long sweeping strokes, the day of her perfection in painted design draws appreciably nearer.

PRACTICE GIVES CONTROL OF BRUSH

So it behooves the student to practice this art in which old-time decorators probably served a six- or seven-year apprenticeship. We of today will require at least two years' experience before we can reproduce their unwavering stroke and masterly execution of line and curve. Does this statement cause our enthusiasm to waver? Not if we love to decorate, for patience and the desire to do our work well, accurately, and quickly are prime attributes of real craftsmen. This does not mean that our first two years of work are spent simply on practice, for few can expend their labor on practice alone, but it *does* mean that constantly, through every design we execute, we take great care to perfect each stroke while laying it on. At first we may do much erasing, so let's keep the carbona bottle handy! But as we increase in experience we will find with delight that our strokes are more and more often turning out to be quite as we wished to have them.

We never attempt a brush-stroke pattern of any kind without a constant singing in our ears of "remember the Japanese artist!" Somewhere in the dim past, we read a story concerning a contest between Japanese artists for a royal prize. One year's time was allowed for the artists to produce their masterpieces. Now the Japanese excel in brush-stroke painting, often contriving to make a single line mean much in form and action. One artist visioned a perfect line six feet long as the most difficult of attainment, so he spent the year practicing toward this end. At last he succeeded in painting a bow, with six-foot cord — fine, straight and unwavering. To him the prize was awarded. Deep in our subconsciousness this story lies, ever an admonition to strive for perfection in brush stroke.

LOADING THE BRUSH

To begin our practice, let us select one of our small three-quarter-inch square-tipped brushes to which we have fitted a short wooden handle. On a palette, or plain piece of paper, squeeze out a little japan tube color, vermilion, perhaps, or chrome yellow. In a small cup (such as the screw top of a catsup bottle), place about a tablespoonful of japan gold size. Dip the brush into the sizing, then dissolve a little of the japan tube paint into the brushful of sizing. Next stroke the brush full length upon a waste piece of paper, observing whether the mixture of paint and sizing is of the desired density. A test stroke of this kind is always pulled toward the decorator. If any lumps of paint or dust are observable on the brush, it is stroked again, its full length, on the paper. When the brush is sufficiently wiped out so that it is carrying just the right amount, and not *too* much, of *flowing paint,* the real brush stroke is attempted.

PRESSURE AIDS BREADTH OF LINE

Useful practice brush strokes are suggested in the sample on page 219. On the upper line are strokes heavy at the left and pulling down to a very fine line. Pressure on the brush is heavy at first, and two-thirds of the hair length is laid on the paper. As the stroke progresses, the pressure is lifted, as well as the brush, so that at the finish of the stroke only a tiny tip of the brush is in contact with the paper.

An S stroke, such as we find in the second line, is started with a tiny tip of the brush, which is pushed downward and obliquely at one and the same time when the stroke approaches the broad middle section of the S. Then this pressure is gradually lifted until only a fine tip is used at the finish. It is hard to describe this variation of pressure, and brush length, but practice will prove enlightening. In general, remember that heavy pressure on a brush will broaden a stroke, release of pressure will lighten the line. So an even line requires even pressure throughout its entire length.

ALWAYS A SQUARE-TIPPED BRUSH

We have selected the three-quarter-inch hair brush, or "pencil" as it would have been called by the old-timers, for its adaptation to perfect brush strokes. As has been said, a longer hair cannot be controlled perfectly from one end to the other, and a shorter one will only accomplish chunky brush strokes. A *square*-tipped brush, with every hair exactly the same length is requisite for smooth brush strokes. A pointed tip, with hairs of graduating length, will not obey the decorator's command, as the shorter hairs will fly out and strike the background surface when least expected. Any broken or short hair in one of our square-tipped brushes will cause the same trouble. If a brush is continually disobeying our commands, it probably has several short hairs that should be removed. Always see that a stroking brush is perfectly flexible *its entire length* before using. It is well to dip it in paint remover for thorough softening, and then carefully wipe out all traces of remover before starting a design.

If a brush is too heavy for a particular design, it may be trimmed down to slenderer proportions by removing outside hairs at the base where they are set into the quill. The professional decorator generally graduates his brushes, from large to fine sizes as the hairs gradually wear or break. If a brush appears to be too heavy for a fine design, do not hesitate to exchange it for a smaller brush. Perfect workmanship depends upon such adjusting of mechanical aids. Make your tools help you, not handicap you. Though they say it is a poor workman who blames his tools, we notice the expert craftsman has *his* carefully selected and suited to his needs.

BROAD STROKES

Insofar as it is possible, most leaf strokes are accomplished with a single laying on of the brush. But occasionally a very wide section appears which must be defined by two strokes, one down each outer edge, and then filled in with one, two, or three full-length center strokes. Do not fuss with many short dabs, which spoil the smooth flow of paint, and interrupt the modeling of form.

MIXING OF PAINTS

No sooner will the student start to mix paints for brush-stroke patterns than she will discover a peculiar translucence in original examples. While vermilion, white and some yellows produce solid flat tones, perfect in background coverage, many greens, blues, reds and other yellows may appear to have been used in a semi-transparent, semi-dense manner. Right here the student should take time out for experimenting upon paper having the same background as the pattern she is reproducing. It will become at once apparent that there are two ways of making a color more transparent. First, it may be paled out by using more sizing or varnish in proportion to pigment, just as water-color paints become pale tones by the addition of more water. Or, secondly, we may try to approximate the color by using more of the pigments which we know are transparent or semi-transparent by nature. Thus, on country tinware, the green strokes used to represent leaves, almost invariably prove to be a combination of Prussian blue and raw umber, mixed with a touch of chrome yellow (mostly opaque) or white (entirely opaque). Verdigris, an early green pigment, transparent by nature, would require raw umber to tone down its brilliance and a touch of yellow ochre to make it register at all over a black background. Chrome yellow light would make it a more opaque light green, while chrome yellow medium would build the coverage up one step more.

Experimentation is the best and quickest teacher. We must learn the old-timers' trick of making paints partially transparent, or we will find ourselves falling short in the perfect reproduction of their workmanship. By the slight transparency of their pigments, they somehow suggested the texture of real flowers, where our modern opaque paints look harsh and blatantly artificial.

CURVED-LINE COMPOSITION

Close study of brush-stroke patterns reveals a wonderful understanding of curve-composition. Almost never do we find a straight line; but time after time we run across patterns where one curve melts naturally and gracefully into other curves, the whole perfectly poised and balanced. Take the two-color pattern on an oval tea-caddy shown on page 220; here we have an asymmetrical design, where curves radiate with easy grace into perfect balance. No straight line enters into the picture, and, we venture to suppose, a *different* curve on almost any section would upset this natural balance. We must learn equal mastership of curved-line composition, if we wish to reproduce the true spirit of our early decorators.

SUPERIMPOSED LIGHT AND DARK TONES

In most simple country designs, superimposed details of light or dark are added twenty-four hours apart, when the first units of the pattern are quite thoroughly set. Occasionally we find a build-up of four or five layers, each of which must be spaced a day apart. For, even though a previously painted unit may *seem* perfectly dry to the finger tips, in less time, a superimposed brush stroke (which necessarily carries gold sizing or varnish) softens the apparently dry under section and starts its dissolving. The only possible exception to this statement is when an experienced decorator lays on the new stroke *quickly and accurately,* with no second touch of the brush and no erasure. Even then there is danger of the stroke "spreading" a little while drying, because of its affinity to the paint lying beneath. It therefore becomes desirable that a decorator carry along the painting of not just one article at a time, but four or five, on each of which he (or she) may accomplish one stage a day. Otherwise the temptation "to just try" the next development becomes overpowering, and the smoothness of a design is ruined.

FINE-LINE STRIPING

Hardest of all brush strokes is the fine stripe found on almost every article of painted furniture. The brush for this work has no handle, and carries hairs one-and-one-half inches long. Paint with which striping is done *must* be mixed with varnish only. If mixed with sizing, the line has a tendency to vary alternately from thick to thin, in flow; while turpentine, oil or any other medium, permits the line to stray from the confines we laid down for it. Varnish that is too old, and has begun to thicken, will make an uneven stripe. A flat-finish background is likely to make a stripe "feather," or grow a fuzzy edge as it dries. For this reason, we generally stripe upon a glossy or varnished surface.

LOADING THE STRIPING QUILL

To practice with a striping brush, we mix a teaspoonful or more of varnish with japan or oil color in a low flat tin. The pigment must be *all* smoothly dissolved in the varnish. Then we dip the striping brush in this mixture, its *entire length*. Next we stroke the brush on waste paper, pulling it toward us, and examining the distribution of paint in the brush. If any lumps are on it, the brush must be wiped again on the paper, for the lump will invariably transfer itself to our stripe. When the brush is properly charged with paint in even distribution, we try laying a stripe one-eighth inch away from the left-hand edge of a straight piece of paper. A straight stripe parallel to an edge is easier to lay than one which follows a rounding surface or a curved edge. A round, or oval, stripe is the most difficult of all, and is best accomplished by swinging in clockwise fashion. It is also easier to carry a stripe within one-half inch of a guiding edge, as the eye can readily spot all deviations within this half-inch space. In time it appears to a striper as though he (or she) develops double vision from this attempt to keep one eye on the stripe and the other constantly on the edge by which he (or she) is guiding. If a stripe is farther than one-half inch away from the edge, a cardboard strip, ruler, or other parallel guide should be laid down for assistance.

In laying a stripe, the position of the hand is important. The striping brush being held between thumb, forefinger and middle finger close to the stripe position, the hand is steadied by the other two fingers as much as possible. Sometimes these two fingers may be "locked" over the outside edge of the article being striped, to act as a parallel guide, but this happens rarely. The muscles of the hand are purposely "frozen" into position to prevent all wavering in the line, and many of us almost hold our breath while each brushful of stripe is being executed. Generally the stripe is laid down the left-hand side of a surface, always pulling toward the decorator's body. On striping the upward curved border of a rectangular tray, however, we often come down the right-hand side, as this direction permits an easier swing at the curved corner. When *curving* a stripe we lift up partially with the brush so that only a fraction of the tip is in contact. Striping an octagonal tray border is often so difficult that on each panel we stop short of the desired length, and then turn the tray around, so as to be always striping from the corner inward toward the center of each side. Trying to join these two halves into a perfect line is "some" stunt!

To aid ourselves, we always tip, tilt and maneuver an object to be striped into a comfortable or advantageous position. Thus a chair is placed on its back, top rail toward the decorator, when striping the upright posts and vertical sections of chair-back panels. Horizontal stripes are accomplished by stepping to the side and pulling a stripe toward each side post or end panel stripe. Critical times are encountered in first laying down the tip of a striping brush, and in finally picking it up at the end of a line, because these two spots generally fall short of the outside edge by one-eighth of an inch or more. When striping the base of a chair, we have it standing upon our work-table, where we twist and turn it in any fashion to facilitate drawing the striping brush toward us. It takes a long while to acquire a fine striping hand, and practice alone achieves this, so let us not be discouraged.

BROAD BANDS

Broad stripes, which we will call bands, to distinguish them from the fine hairline stripe described above, are done by several different methods. They may be laid on with a thick striping brush, but are apt to be unsatisfactory because one side of the line or the other usually spreads out of the desired bounds. Our preference is the double hairline stripe which is filled in by a long sweep of a broad three-quarter-inch hair show-card brush. A beautifully smooth band in bronze results from rubbing on dry bronze powder with a velvet-wrapped finger, just before the striping color sets. But, we must first be certain that there is nothing else sticky in the vicinity which can receive this powder accidentally.

FINE STRIPE NOT OFTEN IN BRONZE

On old furniture and trays we seldom find a fine hairline stripe in bronze, probably because the mixture of varnish with powder is apt to thicken quickly so that an even flow from the brush is next to impossible. Fine stripes of yellow paint are most customary.

CONTRASTING STRIPES

Striping colors generally contrast strikingly with the backgrounds on which they are used. Thus we find black on most light-colored chairs, white or yellow on black chairs, pale yellow on dark green, vermilion or black on very pale green, French blue on pearl gray, black on vermilion, white on a dull dark red, and so on.

Banding colors are apt to reflect some prevailing color in the pattern, to help bring that color down onto other parts of a chair. Some turnings on legs and stretchers are similarly colored for the same reason.

TRANSPARENT BANDS

When doing *transparent* bands on light-colored chairs (such as the common yellow variety), the mixture consists largely of varnish, with just a little tone from some of our partially transparent brown oil colors. Occasionally we find a thin transparent gray band, like a shadow, made with a touch of lamp black in varnish. These transparent trimmings require that the band be put on *all at once* without stopping, so that the varnish may settle itself in perfect position. Never rehandle the transparent band once it is in place. Thus, we should remember that the safest way to stripe and band is upon a varnish-protected surface which will allow any slight erasures. All corrections must be made immediately, if not sooner!

A never-failing source of wonderment lies in the professional and "finished" look a piece assumes when properly banded or striped. Primarily this is due to that first principle of good decorating: namely, that a design should emphasize construction. If a stripe is correctly placed it *follows* the construction absolutely, accenting all edges and high-lighting special places of importance in turnings on legs and stretchers. Let us observe how the old-timers did it! If we record their unfailing sense for decorative accents, we may develop within ourselves a similar ability. For there is no greater teacher in the world than critical observation and accurate remembrance.

PART FOUR

Freehand Bronze Painting

The Three Stages in Painting a Freehand Bronze Rose

Freehand Bronze Painting

REEHAND bronze painting, as the name implies, is a method of applying bronze to a pattern without the use of a stencil or theorem. The pattern first being painted entirely freehand in a sticky composition of pigment and varnish or gold size, it is allowed to become almost dry, and then is made to take high lights of gold, silver or copper bronze powder from a piece of velvet. In freedom from restraint and grace of line, freehand bronze work ranks higher than the more tiresome, repetitious stenciling with which it is frequently combined. In juxtaposition to lustrous gold leaf, the dark, rich tones of bronze work are a clever foil, particularly when used against light or color backgrounds.

Freehand bronze patterns are at least as old as the beginnings of japanning, and we suspect them to be far older than that in true Oriental lacquer. Most pieces of ground work in japanner's designs are done by freehand bronze method, with occasionally just the faintest use of a hillock stencil to define a tiny detail. (See the example on page 238.) Freehand bronze work in infinite variety has been observed on early pie-crust trays of the true Chippendale period, dating from 1750 to 1780. Many rectangular curved-corner trays, heavy in weight and bearing a horizontal flange or border, are known to have intricate use of freehand bronze painting. These may date from 1760 to 1800, possibly the product of true old-time japanners, so laboriously are they executed. We also find freehand bronze details used on rectangular trays with the more usual outcurving border, where they are combined with classic motifs of the Sheraton or Directoire period. Many American Sheraton fancy chairs, dating from 1785 to 1815, will be found to have freehand bronze patterns, but transition types originating between 1815 and 1820 occur with the beginnings of stenciling.

In making such general statements as the above, we are aware that there are always exceptions, and something unexpected may turn up. There are often individual examples due to the idiosyncracies of some decorator, or to the particular difficulties presented by some problem he was trying to solve. In general, however, we feel the foregoing outline is a fair index of the periods in which freehand bronze work was popular.

LAYING IN PATTERNS ON DRY BACKGROUND

Quite contrary to stenciling, freehand bronze work is absolutely dependent upon a perfectly dry background or basic paint. Flat white, flat black, or any color flat finish paint, works admirably; while a background in which there is asphaltum or varnish is apt to give trouble. Various colors are used in the laying of freehand bronze patterns; often the design is painted with lamp black and gold size, sometimes with burnt umber flowed in varnish or in gold size, or with a dull green leaf color mixed with either of these two gummy vehicles. In general, the larger the unit in a pattern, the more likely is varnish to be used as a medium, since even drying qualities over a large area are more obtainable through varnish than through the faster drying gold size. For speed, however, sizing may be used in small spaces. If two bronze-shaded sections of a pattern come directly against each other, they must be executed one at a time, the first to be rubbed with its bronze powder at the proper stage, and allowed to dry completely, before the contiguous section may be started.

SUPERIMPOSED DETAILS

After the bronze has been applied with the same velvet-wrapped forefinger process that we described in the chapter on stenciling, our pattern is given at least twenty-four hours to dry. Then we may apply, one at a time, any small shadings or details that are superimposed. Shaded areas are generally made from varnish and the transparent colors, or from opaque japan colors reduced to a semi-transparent state by being flowed in a plentiful proportion of varnish. Fine line details are usually added the following day; for this purpose japan gold size may be used since time for the careful shading of areas is not required.

BRONZE SECTIONS FOLLOW GOLD-LEAF
UNITS IF USED TOGETHER

When executing a pattern in which both gold-leaf work and freehand bronze are combined, we always *start* with the gold-leaf sections if at all possible. Then after the gold is laid, we proceed with painting the basic colors for the bronze. The reason for this will be obvious when the decorator becomes accustomed to the prime difficulty of laying gold leaf — namely, its tendency to adhere to any spot where it comes in contact with the *slightest* stickiness.

PATTERNS IN CLEAR SIZING

Freehand bronze patterns may be laid in perfectly clear japan gold size or varnish without the admixture of any color, particularly upon a plain black background. So far as making a slightly sticky pattern for the bronze to adhere to is concerned, no color in the mixture is required. But it is difficult to see the transparent gold size distinctly, and in many cases the color used in the size is a necessary part of the design. Freehand bronze patterns done in clear sizing on black backgrounds, are frequently mistaken for stenciling. We must look for the exact repetition of some unit to be sure that the pattern was not done by the freehand method described in this chapter.

FINE HIGH LIGHTS OF BRONZE

Certain expert decorators had a method of handling bronze that almost defies description. Very fine high lights in bronze seem to have been applied with a smaller tool than our velvet finger, perhaps with a charcoal drawing "stump" that is a small roll of curled paper. We may approximate it by applying the bronze powder with a brush moistened in water — or (should I confess it?) saliva! This permits a soft line of gold to be put in its needed position — while the broader clouds of bronze may be added afterward. There is a peculiarly different texture apparent in this bronze line, it in no way resembles a real painted brush stroke. There is a lack of definition, a fuzziness that proves the bronze powder was neither wet nor dry when applied.

LIQUID BRONZE PAINT

We cannot say too strongly that the modern decorator's method of using bronze powder mixed with a fluid such as banana oil or gold sizing to represent gold-leaf work, is not a method of our old-time designers. The smooth brilliance of bronze powders is forever lost by such a procedure, and today's bronze paint lies lustreless and dead. We believe that the powder form was expressly invented to do that soft velvet shading which no liquid paint can achieve. If, for purposes of strict economy, the modern decorator cannot use gold-leaf or freehand shaded bronze patterns, let him at least powder his scrawny bronze paint scrolls afterwards with a piece of velvet and the proper shade of bronze powder in order that all traces of unpleasant brush marks may be removed. In this manner he will most nearly approximate the perfect smooth surface of gold leaf. But, whenever possible, let us leave the *major* use of bronze mixed paint to radiators and other utilitarian objects upon which it is most suitable.

Freehand bronze work in this country undoubtedly met its doom in that dread early nineteenth century period when panics, failures and cut-throat competition caused all fine artistry to decline. It did not persist much after stenciling gained a good foothold in the 1820's. Stenciling lent itself ideally to the business necessity of rapid, quantity production, while freehand bronze remained almost as slow and laborious as gold-leaf work. We view this decline with regret, for freehand bronze work has a charm and appeal that is hard to equal. In the hands of Chippendale and Sheraton master decorators, where classic design, finesse of technique and an inherent appreciation of beauty were incomparably blended, we see freehand bronze work at its very best.

PART FIVE

Methods of Laying Gold Leaf and Similar Metals

Methods of Laying Gold Leaf and Similar Metals

SINCE time immemorial, gold leaf has been used to adorn the finest products of the decorator's art. For costliness of material and intricacy of handling it is considered without equal; while for sheer beauty and elegance it defies all substitutes. Yet gold leaf, beaten to its extreme thinness, is not really expensive and may be handled in various ways that are not very difficult. These methods *must* be learned by all decorators worthy of the name — for no type of ornamenting was so universally used through all periods — yes, even the stencil period!

Gold leaf comes in sheets about four inches square in a number of different shades, but for our purpose we select the rich gold and pale or lemon gold which approaches silver color. Rich gold comes mounted upon loose sheets of tissue paper by which it may be lifted easily. In the decorative trade this is known as gold leaf "for gilding in the wind." Pale gold is difficult to purchase with the same mounting, so we cut squares of wax paper large enough to cover the metal. By laying the paper down carefully upon the pale gold leaf and pressing with the palm or finger tips, the wax melts just enough to make our gold leaf adhere. The same process may be done with silver and other metal leaves, only obtainable in unmounted form.

Old-time methods of making gold leaf were very laborious. The gold was laid between sheets of parchment, bound in a packet, placed on top of a granite post and beaten with a powerful mallet. From time to time as the gold spread, it was subdivided into other layers and beaten again and again until the legal thinness was attained. Now, however, there are mechanical beaters, some of which we regret to say, produce a gold leaf that gives us a porous surface. When we appear to have this kind of gold leaf we change our source of supply to some company that makes a more satisfactory or hand-beaten variety.

The old-time decorators probably used a leather cushion on which to spread their gold leaf for cutting into desired sizes, much as we see the modern window letterer handle his precious metal today. In this case a broad, flat, squirrel-tail brush rubbed against the decorator's hair to become electrified, or to become slightly oily, picks up the cut piece of gold from his leather cushion and transfers it to the sized pattern. However, we get along much better today with our tissue or wax paper sheet for lifting.

In handling a book of gold leaf, let us be careful how we open the pages. Only one tiny corner at a time should be carefully turned while we look for a glimpse of the gold leaf itself. We must not flip the pages wide open to the breeze, for like as not we have picked up a book of unmounted pale gold leaf and the precious stuff will crumple.

PREPARATION OF BACKGROUNDS

Like freehand bronze, gold-leaf work requires an *absolutely dry* background. Two or three coats of flat black paint are excellent, providing they are applied fully twenty-four hours apart so as to be each thoroughly dry. Similarly, gold-leaf patterns work well on any flat surface paint, such as green or vermilion japan color mixed with turpentine and only a bit of varnish but devoid of all linseed oil. Let the decorator become very proficient before attempting to work upon a white or pale yellow background where erasures show so distinctly as to be almost prohibitive. *In any case,* if gold leaf is being laid on a color background, we save some of the original color until the article is complete, ready for the final coats. Because, if any trimming of details or painting out of errors is necessary, this original mixture will be required.

APPLYING LARGE AREAS OF GOLD LEAF

The easiest way to start handling gold leaf is to lay a gold panel or border as background for a design in color. For such a background we take a mixture of japan gold size and varnish, and pale gold bronze powder of about the same color as the leaf we intend to lay. The reason for putting in this bronze is to make the sizing easily visible to the eye and to help fill in the breaks which may exist if our gold leaf does not go on perfectly. We could easily substitute for the bronze any color of paint we wish — indeed, the old-timers often used litharge, or a sort of dull red, as it had a peculiarly happy drying quality and gave a warm glow through the gold-leaf surface.

A table decorated in gold leaf directly on rosewood and mahogany.
Attributed to Duncan Phyfe. Date, 1825-30

If we are doing an extensively wide band around a large tray we do not use any of the fast japan gold size, which might cause parts of the area to dry faster than we can lay the gold. Occasionally, on such an expansive surface we use bronze powder and *varnish* instead of gold sizing, as this allows us still more time for laying the sheets of gold. We now permit this sized area to stand until *almost* dry, even drier than the surface we are accustomed to stencil upon.

APPLYING GOLD LEAF TO SIZING

When the psychological moment arrives, we pick up a sheet of gold leaf on its paper backing, lay it gold side down at the point we first began sizing, and press *gently* behind the gold-leaf tissue with a small piece of velvet (such as we use in stenciling) to remove all possibility of air spaces between the gold and the sizing. Lifting the tissue or wax paper sheet to which our gold was affixed, we move it along to the next adjacent spot, until all the gold is made use of and a new sheet is required. In this fashion we progress all around the sized band, relaying gold whenever cracks or joints appear to be noticeable. If the gold sizing has been cleanly laid there should be a per-fect gold band when polished lightly with the velvet. We must not use a heavy hand behind the velvet or we may mar the smooth beauty of our gold-leaf surface in places where the underlying gold size is a little softer than we realize. To obtain a *perfect* gold-leaf background, we must see to it that all our sizing is spread uniformly thin, with no extra damp or drippy places. Any shreds of gold leaf lying outside the sized area should be wiped away with gentle velvet polishing.

VARNISH PROTECTION

If we are wise, we shall set this piece of work aside for twenty-four hours and then give the entire surface a coat of varnish for protection, otherwise we will not be able to erase slight errors on the gold-leaf background. A dry varnish surface will allow quick erasure with carbona, but unprotected gold leaf will dissolve under the same treatment and disappear.

TYPES OF PAINTING USED ON GOLD-LEAF GROUNDS

Several types of painting are done on gold-leaf backgrounds. Some are executed in opaque color, such as black and white and vermilion; some are done with freehand bronze details and transparent colors; some are even known to have small bronze stencil units on black or transparent color. So we must keep our eyes open if we wish to reproduce *just* the effects we find in old examples. Many gold border trays have spaces laid off in the center of each side for color designs and spaces at each corner for a fancy stripe or fretwork, geometrical enough to strike a nice balance with the pattern sections. Sometimes this order is reversed, with the geometric striping placed in the center of each side.

OTHER METALS

At this point it may be in order to say that occasional patterns have been found laid upon silver-leaf bands or another metal of non-tarnishable quality, which might have been made of tin. Such silver-toned metals were often translated into pseudo-gold by an application of orange shellac or golden-colored varnish for which we would employ several coats of varnish blended with yellow lake and burnt umber. Silver leaf will tarnish even under varnish; aluminum leaf, however, can be counted on to stay clear and shiny.

SUBSTITUTES FOR GOLD LEAF

A word of warning should be said concerning other substitutes for gold leaf which are upon the market today. There are several kinds, all golden in color, but so tough that they will not do the fine work we require of gold leaf. If used in wide areas, a crinkled effect is seen, which is never found in the smooth lustre of fine gold. At three or four cents a sheet (depending upon whether we buy at wholesale or retail) gold leaf is not so expensive but that its beauty is worth the price. Therefore we who wish to take pride in our work cling to the original "gold standard."

GOLD-LEAF PATTERNS

Now for patterns in gold leaf, against a black or colored background, we have simply to paint our design with gold sizing and sure brush stroke in the position we want it. We usually employ the same mixture of half japan gold size, half varnish and a little bronze powder. We try to spread the sizing evenly and thinly, in its absolutely correct position. If an error is made, however, erase immediately with carbona and resize that section at once. The pattern is then allowed to "set" to the required dryness, when we lay a sheet of gold leaf upon it, press lightly with velvet and immediately remove the excess gold leaf with a soft camel's hair brush or the same piece of velvet.

In doing a long gold-leaf pattern, such as a border on a large tray, we often find we cannot progress beyond a certain distance before the first section we laid down begins to get very dry. So we lay gold leaf over the first part which seems ready — *but not completely up to the place we have just been painting* which is sure to be so wet that it will smudge. We must lay gold over only a third or a half, perhaps, then add a similar length to the place where we had been painting border; stop painting, lay another section of gold leaf next to the first, and so on. Doubling back in this manner will be continuously required.

Some gold-leaf borders seem to be a mixture of large units like graceful flowers or bold leaves, intertwined with fine stem lines, tiny leaves and tendrils. Larger areas take a lot longer to dry than tiny ones, so we have found it expedient to tackle these larger ones first, placing them where they balance well upon one section of the border. Then we wind in the curving stem line and fine groups of leaves. In this manner all of the border in one section will arrive at the proper drying point more uniformly. But still *some* doubling back will always be necessary, so we usually paint in the large units on the next section in order that they can start setting.

Of course it is possible to use a slower drying medium, such as a varnish or oil gold size, painting the entire pattern and waiting some hours or days for proper drying. But somehow we have never found this type as smooth or clear-cut; and invariably unforeseen interruptions have caused us to forget the sized pattern until it was too dry to take the gold. So we have adopted our aforementioned policy of working in fast sizing and doubling back for the gold-leaf laying. There is always time to complete this manner of gilding before turning aside to some other task.

The laying of a design in gold leaf brings on a hundred chances for it to stick in other spots besides those where we put our sized pattern. Herein lies the great trouble with gold-leaf work. Sometimes the warmth of the hand, humidity in the weather, or an erasure, softens up some spot in the background so that it has an affinity for the gold leaf. It is exasperating — but getting upset will not allow us to cure the difficulty. We have several devices we turn to in such a dilemma: we may paint out the unwelcome smudge of gold leaf by clever touches of background color; we may erase the offending spot entirely with carbona and set the article aside to be retouched another day when the weather may be more auspicious; or we may succeed in scratching off most of the unwanted gold with a sharp tool.

PROTECTION OF BACKGROUND

Still another trick may be employed to prevent such an occurrence happening in the first place. With a damp cloth, we may put a thin coat of whiting over the area where our gold-leaf pattern is to be laid, and when this has dried, excess powder is rubbed away lightly. Bon Ami (which is mostly whiting in composition) is often more likely to be at hand. Or we may dust the background with talcum powder, as a precaution against gold leaf's exasperating habit of adhering where it is not wanted. Then our pattern may be painted as usual over this film of whiting through which it bites to the solid under-surface. As usual we lay the gold leaf when the pattern is dry enough, wiping off excess gold with our stenciling velvet. We allow the gold-leaf design to harden for several days before removing the now unnecessary whiting with a damp cloth handled very gently. We strongly advise the use of whiting for protection when we are about to put a gold-leaf border on a lace-edge tray (asphaltum surface) or upon any background that is not a perfectly *flat* finish. Also, if gold-leaf work must be done in damp or humid weather, it is well to take this precaution for protecting the background surface.

ETCHING ON GOLD LEAF

Having laid our pattern in japan gold size, and applied the gold leaf as directed, we now have before us a design in one flat tone of gold, unshaded. To give the units form and interest, details are added by several different methods. First, there is the etching into the gold surface with a sharp-pointed stylus or with a group of needles especially designed for this purpose. Etching is more perfect if done within forty-eight hours of laying gold size pattern, and absolutely *must* be done before any over-coating of varnish is applied. By this method midribs and veins curve down the center of a leaf and stamens adorn the middle of a rosette-like flower. Cross-hatching with a single pointed tool is also used to give apparent shadow to gold-leaf areas, particularly on cornucopias. Indeed, this presence of etching is the surest sign a pattern was laid on in gold leaf and was not stenciled in solid bronze.

Occasionally, instead of etching with a sharp-pointed tool, the old-time decorators painted fine black lines in a similar manner. For this we may substitute our "crow quill" drawing pen and Higgins waterproof India ink. But if the ink line starts to "skid" or pull from its original position we abandon this pen method for the fine painted line. (Skidding seems to be caused by an oily residue in the sizing over which we laid our gold leaf.) To paint these fine lines we require a mixture of lamp black in oil and japan gold size, applying it with a very very fine ¾-inch "pencil" or brush. For absolute freedom in this procedure we may have a dry coat of varnish over the gold-leaf work, so that light erasures may be permitted if a line should slip out of control.

SHADING WITH TRANSPARENT COLOR

Next, we find that gold-leaf patterns are frequently shaded with a russet brown tone, partly burnt sienna and raw umber, or else burnt umber, varying with the fancy of the original decorator. Just a touch of this color comes on russet centers, on shadow sides of flower forms, and down the center of leaves. These pigments are flowed on either in varnish or japan gold size, not sooner than twenty-four hours after *painted* black veins and other details, but may be added directly after *etched* lines, wherein there is no pigment to become dislodged. Also after allowing Higgins ink lines to dry about twenty or thirty minutes, we may add our brown varnish shading, since there is no similarity in fluid mediums between the ink and the varnish. Remembering that we can allow ourselves no erasures when working upon unvarnished gold-leaf surfaces, we often hasten to put in the etched lines and then varnish over the pattern before adding the brown shadows. For the beginner we would suggest the use of fine painted lines, since etching may neither be erased nor corrected, unless we wish to lay a new unit of gold leaf over the error.

Whatever course be chosen, always remember that a pattern on which gold leaf is laid must be allowed twenty-four hours to dry before applying any further gold size or varnish. If attempts are made to shade gold leaf with color and varnish too soon, the gold itself will appear to dissolve at the touch of our brush.

One strange thing about gold leaf is that it appears to seal the surface on which it is laid, and any imperfectly dried sizing that lies beneath always stays subject to finger marks. By laying gold too soon we are excluding air from its natural drying action upon the gold size and thereby are suspending its tendency toward drying.

FINE BORDERS ON LACE-EDGE TRAYS

While we have said that gold-leaf work is not too difficult for the beginning decorator, at this point we must confess that there are two exceedingly intricate types of patterns that challenge even the best of us. First of all, I refer to the feathery gold border which lies just within the pierced circumference of a lace-edge tray. We have not yet seen a lace-edge tray without some such border, though frequently, we know, all the gold itself has been washed away and the pattern only reveals itself by a shiny line. (Exception — Once we saw a small tray with such a border done in *three* colors, which proves that gold leaf could not have been intended.) Sometimes, too, we find that the border was laid in a partially transparent dull red, probably achieved by adding litharge to the gold size. We have seen this so many times that the question has arisen whether or not this border was meant to appear dull red in its finished state. But, if we examine carefully, we generally find a glint of gold still clinging in one spot or another where it has not been completely worn away. For in general, most lace-edge trays were not given a protective varnish coat and the fragile gold leaf has been wiped away with repeated washings.

To do these delicate borders we require much practice with a fine ¾-inch quill brush. Here we *must* observe how fluently they broadened the tip end of each leaf stroke if we wish to match the workmanship of these men who were masters! Recently we have been amazed to discover that there were unpierced trays which match lace-edge trays in every other particular, feathery gold border and all! On the back of one of these was painted a strip about three inches long, a sample section of the same gold border appearing on the front. It was as though the decorator had tried out his pattern to get the effect. Or was it, as we have heard, a question of separate artists for each division of lace-edge tray painting — one for the gold-leaf work, one for the scattered flower sprays, and one for the important central unit which must be most perfect of all? Having completed his work, did the floral artist decide which border he wished to have the gold-leaf worker use in this instance?

The other very difficult stunt in gold-leaf work is the executing of fine-line designs with the crow quill pen. Such patterns originated in early japan work and continued to be employed in one form or another by the *most* expert decorators of almost every period up to 1850. The problem has to do with finding a medium that will flow properly from a fine pen point. We have always had difficulty in making either varnish or japan gold size work with the crow quill pen. But raw linseed oil will flow, if care be taken not to overload the pen. Use this method against a flat paint background, or against a surface that has been protected with whiting. Allow the oil lines to dry in a protected place from three to six days before laying the gold leaf upon them. The linseed oil must have sufficient time to oxidize and become almost dry, so that the laying of gold leaf (or of bronze powder) upon the hardening oil will not cause smudging. Careful testing with the finger should help the decorator decide when the psychological moment for laying the gold leaf has arrived.

While the pen-and-linseed-oil process works well on a flat paint background, it also clings nicely to a glossy or varnish surface without skidding. But, if by any chance, the pen-and-linseed-oil lines *should* take to *spreading* when applied to a flat paint background, we know then there is some oiliness present in the ground paint, and we must change our method. Again, a non-oily method must be employed if we are copying an old design onto traceolene or other tracing paper which allows the line to spread.

GUM ARABIC

Following a hint in an old-time painting book, we started experimenting with gum arabic to find a sizing which would fill our requirements. Gum arabic crystals were allowed to stand in water twice their depth for several days. The resultant mixture was then strained and experimented with for thickness and for diluting materials. One set of directions called for the addition of sugar; another for wine; and the results in each case were quite satisfactory. We then proceeded to add maple syrup (which we remember as being very sticky), and the last mixture was placed in our paint-basket, stoppered well in a small bottle. Some weeks afterward we were startled to hear a hissing noise like steam issuing forth from the paint-basket; its cause being the fermenting of our maple syrup in the gum arabic! By this time our mixture refused to flow well from the pen; so we abandoned that novelty as impractical.

Now that our excursion in experimenting has come to a close we have settled down with a solution of gum arabic, sugar and water with a little wine, just thin enough to flow from a pen. Perhaps the wine assists in drying the lines more rapidly. A bright yellow water-color tube paint is added to make the mixture more visible. According to the old books, we allow the gum arabic lines to dry, then breathe heavily upon them to revive a suggestion of stickiness before laying our gold leaf. Heaven help us if we use this mixture on a painted tray and anything in the background revives to stickiness also! However, used upon a flat painted ground, when linseed oil has previously shown a tendency to spread, this gum arabic method should be quite successful. It cannot be counted upon to work on a glossy surface or varnished ground at any time.

Occasionally we find patterns where fine pen lines were touched with dull gold, copper, or fire-colored bronze powders, instead of gold leaf. Two reasons for this might be advanced; first, that much good gold leaf was wasted when used over these tiny lines; second, that the duller bronze coloring was selected for contrast to the matchless brilliance of gold leaf.

Our early japanners must have had some fluid they applied with a pen before laying tiny gold-leaf or bronze patterns. But we have searched that extravagantly worded volume on japanning, published in 1688, by Stalker and Parker, from cover to cover without tracking down any information on this most intricate side of their art. Perhaps they were reserving this particular secret for their own protégées and themselves — who knows?

LAY GOLD-LEAF SECTIONS FIRST

Decorations wherein gold-leaf units comprise only a part of the design, should be begun by laying those gold-leaf sections first. Otherwise our gold may adhere to undesirable places in nearby bronze or color work where a bit of stickiness may linger. Gold leaf thus accidentally adhered is difficult to paint out or otherwise remove without damaging adjoining sections of our pattern.

GOLD-LEAF GROUNDS FOR TRANSPARENT COLOR

Once in a great while we find gold- or silver-leaf areas used as a background to reflect light through transparent or semi-transparent colors, just as sunshine gleams through stained-glass windows. Thus we find glowing deep red roses and rosebuds applied over a gold-leaf base and high-lighted with overtones of golden bronze powder. Again, iridescent birds of paradise owe their gleaming colors to a foundation of gold or silver leaf when applied over a golden bronze background. But this use of clear radiant color belongs more to the following chapter than to our present subject of gold-leaf work.

Difficult and annoying as the art of laying gold leaf may be, the permanence of its beauty more than compensates for the trouble involved. Speed and accuracy in the application of the gold sizing help the decorator to avoid many pitfalls that we have enumerated.

Thus, once we have mastered knowledge concerning the materials and methods of our craft, we should work for developing a perfection of line and leaf stroke, that we may proceed without errors and erasures. For, above all things, we must master the technique of gold-leaf work if we would have at our fingertips the method which for sheer beauty and lasting satisfaction is without a near rival.

PART SIX

Technique of Floating Color

Technique of Floating Color

TO CONFESS the truth, we have coined the above phraseology to describe a curious method of flowing transparent color overtones upon an underlying form or pattern. A coat of varnish is painted over the design, and into this our transparent color is shaded broadly with a fair-sized brush. Particles of this color are spread by the varnish through its usual process of leveling and setting. In this manner all sharp lines are blurred and softened into subtle shading, and are made to melt away into nothingness where we leave the varnish clear.

Floating color is not a technique to be used by itself, for the results would be only cloudy sugestiveness of the pattern. It is merely a secondary shading of a rose, a morning glory, or a bird's breast and wing, where, on succeeding days, finishing brush strokes are touched in to make the design more definite.

Just as stained glass must have daylight to reveal its jewel-like beauty, floating color depends upon the reflection of light *through* it from the underlying form or pattern. This light comes in varying degrees from an opaque pigment such as white, vermilion, gray, green — in fact anything short of black, which *has* no light to give back through the transparent overtone. Color so applied is fascinating in the clarity and blending of its rainbow hues and is mysterious to the uninitiated decorator who does not understand the difference between pigments that are transparent or are opaque by their own nature.

In explanation, let us compare two ways a rose might be painted. A modern designer takes white paint into which he works varying amounts of red to make the shades of pink required. Deep pink or almost red may be used in the deep "cup" of the inner rose, light pink or almost white may be used on high-lighted petals. This result, withal, is apt to look very thick or "pigmenty." Now, by our floating color methods, the rose may be painted quite flatly in a light soft shade of opaque pink, flowed on in japan gold size or varnish. (This is *expected* to look "pasty.") *The next day,* a coat of clear varnish is applied to the exact form of our rose and transparent alizarin crimson is worked into the deeper shaded sections of flower "cup" and shadow petals. This is allowed to dry twenty-four hours while the color diffuses itself slightly in the setting varnish. Lastly, on the *third* day, we apply those light feathery overtones of white, made semi-transparent by admixture of gold size or varnish, that veil the rose so delicately. These strokes must hold their shape and position — and so must *not* be applied while the previous floating color is still damp. A rose painted in this manner is fascinatingly different from the pasty-colored flower first described.

WHITE AS A BASIS FOR COLORS

Oftentimes, particularly on a dark background, white is used as a basis upon which to build floating color. Thus we have copied bleeding-hearts painted first in flat white, and on the second day have given them a coat of varnish (in their own form) into which we tinged alizarin crimson at the base. We have seen small forget-me-nots painted in two tones of white, a semi-transparent tone in which more definite white pigment was placed for form and high light. Over this flower on the following day the decorator flowed varying tones of blue, violet and green, made from our transparent colors of Prussian blue, mauve and verdigris. (Of course any transparent color that was too brilliant might have been tamed down with a touch of raw umber.) Still another day must have been allowed to pass by for the addition of a dot of opaque yellow to the center of these forget-me-nots. One would think the story ended here, but as a matter of fact, on a still subsequent day, the decorator added a tiny touch of alizarin crimson to accent the yellow center. Surely there were no limits, sometimes, to the patience of a decorator who used floating color for shading. And we must admit that there is nothing to compare with the clarity of color, the vibrant quality of paint which this flowed-on-in-varnish method produced.

GOLD- OR SILVER-LEAF BASE

As previously stated, a gold-leaf base was occasionally used to reflect the light which floating color requires. If against a black background we see a rose or rosebud glowing in a rich *transparent* red, we may guess that gold leaf is responsible. Once in a while we find silver leaf behind clear blue units, which would become too green when used over gold.

On lace-edge trays the central or important flower motif is often shaded with transparent floating color. For instance, we find a tulip painted first in varnish and opaque ivory white (Phillips white with yellow ochre and raw umber) into which occasional streaks of dull blue are worked. Then on the following day, a clear covering of varnish is placed over the tulip and is tinged with alizarin crimson, a little yellow lake or clear Prussian blue. The result is a strikingly clear-toned blossom which throws its beauty across a forty-foot room.

A semi-transparent variation of floating color is found in lace-edge tray examples of the peach, where the first coat is a definite body of vermilion shaded with raw umber and burnt umber. The following day our coat of clear varnish is put on, tinged with alizarin crimson, raw umber, burnt umber and Prussian blue, which are transparent colors, but the opaque paints of white, yellow ochre and a French blue (where white and Prussian are combined) are used in higher-lighted portions. The shading of such a peach on a lace-edge tray may consume from thirty to forty-five minutes!

TRANSPARENT COLORS OVER STENCILS

In one sense the transparent colors we flow on over bronze stenciled units might be termed floating color. For this too, varnish is selected as the vehicle because we know it will level out more smoothly than the faster-drying medium, japan gold size. In later years, around 1840 or 1850, highly-colored metallic bronzes were placed upon the market, thereby dispensing with the necessity of coloring by a second-day bit of handwork. But here we are digressing from the subject at hand.

AN OLD ART

The process of floating color is at least as old as the introduction of japanning, when many of the colors available were distinctly transparent in make-up. Against the dark background of most japan work, transparent colors would be absolutely ineffectual, unless defined by light-reflecting patterns. Connecticut chests and boxes of the "Guilford" type have given evidence of transparent reds, greens, yellows and browns used in a semi-floating manner upon heavy white patterns. These decorators, too, had the same problem of working upon dark backgrounds where their pigments were not individually effective.

Floating color, then, as we observe it, is a dreamy manner of blending transparent tones over an underlying pattern. It is generally found on the most intricate products of the decorator's art, as though only the masters understood their pigments and vehicles sufficiently to achieve this indirect shading. Needless to say, the main floral motifs were generally done in floating color, that by their jewel-like brilliancy they might attract more attention than other parts of the design.

PART SEVEN

The Early Art of Japanning

The Early Art of Japanning

INASMUCH as no term has been used to cover more types of work than the word "japanning," a history of its definition might be here in order. Originally, it covered the art of English craftsmen who imitated Oriental lacquer work during the 16th, 17th, and 18th centuries, thereby making furniture look as if it were "made in Japan." In the earliest days there was no definite recognition of the fact that many other pieces of lacquered furniture came from China and India. Thus the one term "Japan" was sufficient to represent the entire Orient to most English minds. Chippendale, as we know, turned to the Chinese for much inspiration, and yet the pieces he designed for a painted finish were specified as "suitable for japanning." In America, vast numbers of our Sheraton fancy chairs were advertised as "japanned," though we doubt if, by this late time, any Oriental characteristics were present in the decorative design. About the year 1800, the word "japanned" gradually gave way to the term "fancy," applied alike to wood, cane, or rush seat chairs, as if it meant simply, "painted with an ornamental design." Yet the word "japanned" has clung to metal trays and other small articles of painted tin from 1780 even up to the present time. It now refers to those shiny brown bread tins and cake boxes we find in the kitchenware sections of department stores. By this time we suspect that "Japanned Ware" simply refers to tin which has been coated with asphaltum and placed in a drying or annealing oven for hardening.

So let us return to the earliest form of the word japanning and consider the art of those early craftsmen who were really trying to work in Oriental style. We used to suppose that the American Colonies imported their japanned furniture from England but we have found much evidence that Nehemiah Partridge, japanner, was working in Boston as early as 1711, and eight or nine similar craftsmen resided in this same city between that date and 1770. Sad to relate, many of these skilled decorators died insolvent, unable to make a living by the intricate methods they employed.

But the story of how japanning was done in those days should begin with the direction book by Stalker and Parker, published in England in 1688. Such flowery speech and such extravagant claims for the art of japanning we shall never meet again. In their introduction we read:

"Well then, as Painting has made an honourable provision for our Bodies (in preserving portraits that are true to life) so Japanning has taught us a method, no way inferior to it, for the splendor and preservation of our Furniture and Houses. These Buildings, like our Bodies, continually tending to ruin and dissolution, are still in want of fresh supplies and reparation. On the one hand, they are assaulted with unexpected mischances, on the other with the injuries of time and weather; but the Art of japanning has made them almost impregnable against both: no mouldering worm, or corroding time can possibly deface it; and which is much more wonderful, although its ingredients, the gums, are in their own nature inflammable, yet this most vigorously resists the fire, and is itself found to be incombustible. True genuine Japan, like the Salamander, lives in the flame and stands unalterable, when the wood which was imprisoned in it is utterly consumed . . . What can be more surprising than to have our chambers overlaid with Varnish more glossy and reflecting than polisht marble? No amorous nymph need entertain a Dialogue with her Glass, or Narcissus retire to a Fountain, to survey his charming countenance, when the whole house is one entire speculum. To this we subjoin the Golden Draught, with which Japan is so exquisitely adorned, than which nothing can be more beautiful, more rich or majestick. Let not the Europeans any longer flatter themselves with the empty notions of having surpassed all the world beside in Stately Palaces and costly Temples and Sumptuous Fabricks. Ancient and Modern Rome must now give place: the glory of one country — Japan alone, has exceeded in beauty and magnificience all the pride of the Vatican at this time, and the Pantheon heretofore; Japan can please you with a more noble prospect, not only whole towns but cities too are there adorned with as rich a Covering; so bright and radiant are their Buildings, that when the Sun darts forth his lustre upon their golden Roofs, they enjoy a double day by the reflection of his beams.

Of course, such extravagant terms surpass all possibility of being lived up to; and the book has recently been described as a "snare and a delusion" written by "two charlatans"! Yet to be perfectly honest, we have found recorded on its pages true directions on how to do many *parts* of japan work. Materials listed are, for bronze powders —

"Brass dust, commonly called gold dust (the best is made in Germany). Silver dust. Green gold. Dirty gold dust. Powder Tinn and Copper. Then is also used in japan work metals, commonly called Speckles of Divers sorts, as Gold, Silver, Copper, and

Two views of a japanner's paint box, showing his dry paints in original hand-blown bottles. Probably American about 1750. Owned by the Author

many other Colours, some finer than others and worked according to the fancy of the Artist, either on Mouldings, the out or in-side of Boxes, drawers, etc."

Undoubtedly "Speckles" are those larger flakes of metal which we now call "Flitters."

From among other items we gather many interesting bits of information, many clues as to just how the early japanners did their work. For instance:

"First some colours we call transparent; such as those we lay upon Silver, Gold or some light Colour and then they appear in their proper colours very beautiful and lively. Of these for your use is first, Distilled Verdigreece for Green, fine Lake for a red, fine Smalt for a blew. . . . Imitation of Tortoise Shell laid upon Silver foil is made use of for cabinets and boxes."

We might add here, this identical process of imitation tortoise shell is found upon many lace-edge trays where fiery high lights smoulder beneath the dark background.

Stalker and Parker continue by directing how to do the "Golden Draught" or delineation of figures and landscapes —

"When you have wrought your work, and that which you intend to decipher on it; draw this (gold) size all over that part, and that part only, which you resolve shall be guilded or adorned with gold, passing over those places where you think to lay your other metal or colours, as copper, silver, or the like. Your size being thus wrought for the Gold, let it stand till it is so dry that when you put your finger upon any of it, it may be glutinous or clammy, and stick a little, but not so moist that the least spot or speck should come off with your fingers, not unlike to thick glue when it is half dry. When you find it agrees with the characters we have given you, conclude that to be the critical minute, the very nick of time, wherein you must apply your Gold; then take a piece of soft washt leather or the like, this being wrapt about your forefinger, dip it into your gold dust, and rub where the gold size is laid, for it will stick on the size and nowhere else. If any dust of gold lies scattered about your work, with a fine Varnishing brush that hath not been used, brush or wipe it all into your gold paper. This being thus finished, take your pencil in hand again; draw that part which you design for Copper with gold size also; and when dry, cover it with Copper, after the same method that you received for Gold. A third time wield your pencil, and lay size for silver, and operate as aforesaid; so likewise for all dead metals, wheresoever you design them. Only take this remark along with you, that you lay your metals successively one after another, suffering each to dry and be covered before you begin a distinct one; as for instance your gold size must be dry and gilded before you proceed farther and so the rest.

"Now when your work expects to be adorned with Rocks, Flowers or the like, use first your Pencil to varnish those places with, and whilst it is wet put some of your strewings into the Sieve (made from an apothecary's box with bottom made of coarse matting) and gently shake it over the place designed for your Rock, until it appears answerable in Speckles to what you intended; but especially when for Rocks, call for a pencil about the size of your finger, one that is drie and new, and with it sweep all those straggling

Speckles that lie beyond the wet or varnished part into the side and top of the Rock that is moistened; for there it will not only stick but render your work, thick with Speckles in those places, more beautiful and oblige it with a kind of Shadow and reflection.

"This work admits of no idle hours, no interludes and vacations, for as soon as one part is completed, the other desires to undergo the skill and contrivance of the artist. When this Rock is drie, the next must succeed in operation; and by this way of working the one, when, and not before, the other is perfectly drie, you may, like the giants of old fighting against Jupiter, cast mountain upon mountain, lay one rock upon or beside another, of different colours, and as many shapes until the whole enterprise of Rock work is completed.

"To make the raised work in imitation of Japan and other paste, . . . you must provide a strong Gum Arabick water; charged with a *double quantity* of Gum. Have in readiness an ounce of Whiting and a quarter of an ounce of the finest and best Bole Armoniack; make them thin enough that it may but just drop from the stick; if too thick gum water will relieve it; if too thin, add more Whiting and Bole Armoniack. The stick that I spake of before should resemble that of a Pencil Stick, but it must have a more sharp and taper end. This dipt into your paste, drop on the Rock, Tree, Flower or House which you propose to raise, and by repetition proceeding until it is raised as high and even as you think convenient. This done, three or four small instruments must be procured; one of them a bended graver, which the Engravers make use of; the rest, small pieces of Steel in shape like a Chissel of the Carpenters, fastened in a wooden handle. With these your raised work must be cut, scraped and carved, leaving one part higher than the other, keeping due regard to the proportion of the thing you design.

"But here I must forewarn you, let no heavy rustick hand be employed in this tender dilligent work; for if in haste or unadvisedly you attempt it, believe me your raised work will break off in several places, to the disgrace of the artist and deformity of the piece. Let therefore your tools have an exquisitely sharp and smooth edge."

We quote thus at length from Stalker and Parker's book on japanning not only because it is the earliest documentary evidence of how Englishmen did japan work, but also because the directions, couched in their quaint language, are still clear, direct, and possible to follow. The only omission seems to be the mention of a sizing which will flow from a pen for applying tiny blades of grass, leaves on trees and similar infinitesimal details. While it is possible to paint hairlines with a very fine brush, we find such a tool impractical from the standpoint of time involved. A fine drawing pen is much more efficient and gives more uniform results.

SIMPLE JAPAN WORK

The *simplest* japan work designs started out as any of our gold-leaf patterns, with Chinese men and women, weeping willow trees and exotic pagodas laid in japan gold sizing with a tiny brush. At the proper time, these patterns were overlaid with gold leaf. Next, pieces of ground work were painted in with clear varnish or with lamp black and gold size, after the freehand bronze method, and allowed to become almost dry. Shading of these bits of land was accomplished in three ways — occasionally by a tiny stencil of wavy lines; often by freehand touching with a piece of wash leather (we would use velvet nowadays) and bronze powder; rarely by that hit-or-miss sprinkling of angular flakes of bronze, called speckles in the old days but now known as flitters. Twenty-four hours later, fine bronze details may have been drawn in by dipping a pen in raw linseed oil.[1] The oxidation of this oil pattern required four or five days, depending on the weather, before touching with wash leather and bronze powder. If the pen-drawn lines appear as bright as gold leaf, then we know they did not apply bronze powder, but indulged in the extravagance of laying gold leaf on the linseed oil penmanship. Last of all, details of features, costumes, etc., were drawn in to complete the picture.

RAISED JAPAN WORK

While the foregoing type of japan work was frequently done in England and America, the *finer* grade consisted of *raised* figure-work. In a japanner's paint kit we have found a mixture of linseed oil and whiting which must have been used for the building up of raised units. Stalker and Parker's directions, as we have seen, called for gum arabic, whiting and bole armoniack. We could employ liquid glue and whiting with the same degree of success, inasmuch as this mixture might cling more tenaciously to the background. (Few craftsmen today would take the trouble to model or carve their raised figure work with engraver's tools as suggested by Stalker and Parker.)

Next, gold leaf was laid upon the raised surfaces, usually over a coat of red sizing so that a warm glow is felt beneath the metal leaf. On so many elaborately japanned pieces both pale and rich gold leaf were used in contra-distinction to each other. Faces frequently were done in the paler shade while the costumes were in the more orange tone of rich gold leaf.

SIDE DESIGNS INFERIOR

On japanned case furniture, such as highboys and lowboys made in the American Colonies, we usually find a very inferior grade of decorative design applied on the two sides. In this position there is little or no gold leaf

[1]See description under gold-leaf work, page 83.

99

used; the pattern is apt to be very coarse and badly drawn in something like bronze *paint* (probably a mixture of bronze powder and gold size). A clumsy wavering stripe is often found as a frame around each end panel. If we are restoring an antique of this kind, where inferior japanning is absolutely evident on the sides, we are in honor bound not to discard it for the finer sort of workmanship accorded the front panels.

In searching about for a reason why the end panels should have been so slighted we gain the impression that the japanner's apprentice was allowed to try his skill here where it does not attract much attention. The master himself, even working hurriedly, could not have drawn quite so badly! Harassed by the grim specter of debts and by the costliness of his time and materials, the japanner may well have thought it necessary to confine his own efforts and his gold leaf to the frontal section of case furniture.

In allowing coarser workmanship on any part of a japanned piece the decorator violated that section of Rule III which pertains to *scale* or relative size. We cannot help but feel the lack of unity in the design when viewing such a piece obliquely.

EMBRACED ALL TECHNIQUES

Reviewing this chapter it will be seen that most of the decorative methods which were later brought into great prominence had their inception in the japanner's imitation of Oriental lacquer. Strange, isn't it, that those odd bits of land and rocks found beneath Chinese pagodas, or strolling mandarins, should carry the earliest beginnings of stencil and freehand bronze work? Transparent color also is described by Stalker and Parker. So, perhaps we can gain an understanding of why the word japanning was broad enough to represent in later years all sorts of decorated furniture and tinware.

PART EIGHT

Searching for an Old Design
Beneath Outer Paints

Searching for an Old Design
Beneath Outer Paints

WHEN old designs have been obliterated by successive layers of paint, we have before us a chance to indulge in an exciting archeological adventure. Undoubtedly we will meet with varying degrees of success ranging from the perfect revelation of a beautiful design to the disappointing discovery that some decorator before us had scraped away all original paint. In between these two extremes are the average cases of finding traces of a damaged pattern, or proof that the article was originally very plainly finished with little more than a band or stripe. Still, search we must, for within our grasp we may hold a precious inheritance which demands our recording. Through the discoveries made in careful investigation work under Victorian or modern paint, we frankly admit that a large part of our knowledge was acquired. Furthermore, we know of collectors who eternally regret having turned over certain antiques for refinishing to a craftsman who thoughtlessly scraped through all layers of paint, without looking for an original pattern. Even if we get no monetary return for the added effort, let us decorators charge it up to experience, but let us *investigate anyway!*

TRYING VARIOUS SOLVENTS

The uncovering procedure is largely experimental, due to the widely varying make-up of paints used in the past one hundred or two hundred years. What will dissolve the outer paints in one case will not work at all in many other attempts. The white enamel paint of twenty years ago resists alcohol rubbing, and holds out bravely against paint remover for hours. Yet in other cases alcohol is too strong for safe usage. It is well to take an inconspicuous place on the article to be investigated where various degrees of solvents may be safely tried out. We might take the back of a chair leg and, starting with alcohol, attempt to discover what color the chair was painted originally. If it was the type often found in a two-toned or grained finish, we keep in mind the two color combinations used for that purpose. If it is found that alcohol works well (and it often does) we should then proceed with it in some such minor design-carrying part (where there is a duplicate on the other side of the chair) like the side post or stile. Any form of liquid remover like soap and water, alcohol, commercial paint remover, etc., does not work well if the outer paints are much cracked or chipped, since the fluid eats into the lower surfaces too rapidly through the cracks.

The solvents we use are here listed in order from mildness to harshness —
> Ivory soap and water
> Naphtha soap and water
> Mechanic's soap (with pumice) and water
> Webber's cleaning fluid for oil paintings
> Denatured alcohol
> Paint remover and steel scraper
> Benzine
> Ether

CHIPPING

Oftentimes we find that instead of using one of these solvents a slow chipping process achieved by the point of a razor blade or pen knife is more desirable. This is particularly true in the case before mentioned where the outer paint surfaces are much cracked or broken away. The success of chipping is due to the tendency of paints not to cling tenaciously over other paints of different chemical construction. Then, too, we believe that many original decorations were covered with varnish or shellac, a slippery surface, which quickly causes outer paints to let go when attacked with an instrument. Once in a while a broader use of the steel scraper will force paints apart at this original shellac level.

KEEPING NOTES

We should keep paper and pencil handy while excavation is going on, so that we may record whatever comes to light *as soon as it makes itself known,* for further attempts at investigation have been known to destroy that which we saw in earlier stages. If all goes well and we completely uncover a distinct design, we may allow the paint to dry out and then take an accurate tracing.

Sheraton fancy chair revealing original design after the
chipping off of outer coats
of paint.

Courtesy of Mrs. A. Edward Ellis

Below: Original design is
shown in the bright tin of
this tray after the removal
of all paint.

When we attempt to uncover an old pattern *and leave the original paint intact,* preparatory to restoring, we enter upon a job worthy of museum experts. We must employ the slower solvents gradually, ever watchful that we do not go too far. Museum pieces merit such expenditure of effort, but the average antique would hardly repay the cost involved. In some cases we have spent eight or nine hours with soap and water washing a small tin box to remove two coats of paint obliterating a design over which (we felt sure) no varnish finish had ever been used. Alcohol as a solvent would then have gone through the decorative design as well as the outer coats of paint.

In any case, we always use a counteracting fixative when the outer paint removal is complete. With chairs, boxes and tinware that were originally finished in varnish, we varnish again, fill in the missing spots and finish with two more coats of varnish. The last coat should be rubbed down with pumice and oil. For Pennsylvania, Connecticut and Taunton chests, where oil paint is usually considered the only proper finish, we put on a coat of raw linseed oil as a counteracting fixative after the outer paint removal is completed. A week or more is allowed for the oil to sink in and revive the original paint. Next we replace all damaged spots with matching paints, allowing them at least a week to harden. Last of all we oil the chest again, a process that should be repeated once a year, if we wish to keep perpetual vitality in the original paint. Even museums exhibit valuable decorated chests with paint rapidly pulverizing and disappearing, in spite of the fact that they at least should know the value of "feeding." When raw linseed oil is first rubbed on with a soft piece of cheesecloth, the chest will look dark and shiny as if varnished, but in the course of several weeks the oil will be absorbed by the hungry paint background, while the glossy effect will gradually disappear. Pieces that are really varnished do not require yearly oiling.

FAINT TRACES EVEN WHEN ORIGINAL PAINT IS GONE

Every once in a while there is a chance of learning something about an original design even though all the paint has been scraped away. This apparent paradox is due to the fact that occasionally the silhouette of a pattern is "photographed" faintly upon the background. The chances are that this object stood in a room where sunlight habitually fell across the design, taking unequal effect upon the underlying wood fibres. Then, too, on many decorated tin objects where the background paint was not heavily laid, we may find a representation of the original pattern, even though no paint remains. In this case we will see the design in shining tin against a background of duller or more rusted tin surface. We feel that the decorative design was an added layer of protection and thus preserved the tin in brighter condition beneath its exact position. When we see a shiny pattern of this kind we will have to draw upon our own experience to decide whether the design was a stencil or a brush-stroke pattern in color. And we will undoubtedly have to supply small details to perfect the pattern.

POOR DESIGN MAY BE SCRAPPED

Now there is one paragraph we hate to write — yet somehow we cannot escape doing it. The truth is, that if we find an old design unworthy of being reproduced we do not always repaint it! We make a record, to ease our conscience, but if the pattern is thoroughly bad we select from our repertoire another pattern which will be both authentic and attractive to the possessor. Still, the decision to throw out an old pattern should be carefully weighed by an expert, since novices are often wrong in their judgment. Not all old-time decorators were great masters of their craft, though the percentage of failures, compared to modern times, was extraordinarily low. Yet somehow we feel there is no necessity to pass on bad art to posterity when we happen upon a thoroughly unsuccessful example.

Of course we are *not* referring to primitives or very early crude examples made during a period when craftsmanship had just begun to develop. These antiques very often fall within the realm of museum pieces — crude though they may be — because of their rarity. And, of course, certain very late style pieces, built during the period of universally bad art, would look incongruous with a design much too fine and early for them. So we write the foregoing paragraph in fear and trembling, yet hoping that we will not be misunderstood. For the truth is, if we dare to scrap a thoroughly poor design, we replace it with a suitable and attractive one *from the same period.* Any student who wishes to shift into patterns of another date does so at his own risk! For invariably, the only repainting that "rings true" is a pattern exact in period with the article's construction.

Thus, in the search for original patterns underneath outer coats of paint, the student acquires not only knowledge but also a new obligation, that of keeping faith with the original decorator! When a worthwhile design comes to light, we report immediately to the owner of the antique concerning our discovery and our opinion of its fitness for restoring or reproducing. We believe the owner should be given the facts, and allowed a chance to have a real reproduction of the original if he wishes to pay for it. Nine times out of ten the owner *will* wish for a faithful copy of the original and will succumb to our persuasion. Occasionally the owner will accept the idea of having the original pattern, but if his heart was set on a black and gold chair he may not wish to have the white and gold finish we found during our excavation. For the sake of peace we may have to compromise upon a black background, while reproducing the original decoration as discovered, and in this case we must content ourselves with the knowledge that the same chairmaker undoubtedly turned out black, red, green and other colored chairs beside the white example we discovered. After all, original pattern is far more important than the background color upon which it was embellished.

Changing of background color is not so simple if the pattern discovered happened to be a stencil one. As we have learned, fine bronze stencil designs depend upon a dark background, and if the owner desires a light color, then a black panel must be supplied.

PART NINE

Restoration and Reproduction of
Original Designs

Restoration and Reproduction of Original Designs

ONCE the question of authenticity is decided, how shall we proceed to restore an object where the original pattern is damaged and yet clear enough to give us an idea of the early decorator's workmanship? The answer is difficult, for it depends jointly upon the degree of damage, the rarity of the original, and the practical problem of how much costly effort will be required to rebuild the original appearance. Here, judgment on the part of the decorator will enter in, and since there are as many variations in judgment as there are types of people in this world, the results will be widely different.

Before going to a lot of trouble in restoring an old pattern we should be absolutely certain that the design really is original, for it would be useless to spend many hours in preserving a pattern that is not antique at all, and does not "belong." How can we be sure? Long and careful study of original methods will develop in us an ability to recognize true antique workmanship. Frequently, we may have seen other examples of this decorator's work. We learn to look for sure brush strokes and the masterly handling of paints by the methods outlined in Part III of this book. We become doubtful of poor technique, and hesitant, wavering lines. We also learn to recognize the styles of design work that were natural to different sorts of antiques because of their construction dates. Long acquaintanceship in the handling of antiques seems to develop a sixth sense in us, and we have a feeling that something rings true or false.

CLEANING AND VARNISHING

Ideally speaking, we believe that the original should be judiciously cleaned with soap and water, or with alcohol, like a painting or canvas, to remove all dirt and overlay of bad shellac; given a coat of varnish, and then touched in only where the original pattern and background are missing. These new touches usually have to be artificially aged by overtones of transparent color so that they match the remaining original sections.

If the cost of this procedure is not too great, we would recommend it always. On our own restorations of originals, we have applied it without exception, regardless of time consumed. For the original paint is far more valuable than any bits of pigment we may add, and should be carefully preserved. If the original paint is somewhat worn in appearance, we may even go so far as to artificially wear down our new sections in order that the entire piece may seem homogeneous. Otherwise, it would become necessary to completely retouch the worn decoration and background, a procedure which would distinctly impair the value of a rare piece.

COMPLETE RETOUCHING

When the original paint is so far gone as to *demand* complete retouching anyhow, we have a choice between two procedures. For one, we may build in the background paint again, directly over the original, leaving the traces of the design wherever visible. When the background is dry, we may then proceed to paint the pattern in its original brilliance of color upon its identical position. By the time we have finished with the dull overtones of antiquing we have a product that is all new paint, but matches line for line the original decorator's workmanship. This first method of procedure has the advantage of *saving* and not scraping away what traces there may be of the original paint, although the resultant finish may be a little rough as to surface.

REPRODUCING OF ORIGINAL

The second method of procedure when an antique decoration is very far gone is to remove the old finish entirely *after* having made a perfect painted record on tracing paper of everything that had been even faintly visible. By removing the badly damaged original, we will achieve ultimately a much smoother finish. Then we repaint the design from our tracing paper record, and supply from our own imagination or research any sections of pattern that may have been missing in the damaged original. It is fun to see if we can design in the manner characteristic of the old-time master himself. To do so we analyze what remains of his workmanship and try to find a solution that might have evolved from *his* mind as well as our own. There were so many variations in types of decorators that this is a challenge to our versatility and inventiveness. In the end, though, we must confess that this method of entirely repainting on a scraped surface should be called *reproducing* an original rather than *restoring*.

Right here we divulge a method we may use as a guide to replacing a design in its identical position, when we will have to scrape away all traces of original paint. (This is, of course, in a case where we have found a damaged pattern, but for purposes of gaining a smooth surface we intend to reproduce rather than to restore the original decoration.) Before obliterating the fragments of old pattern, we take a sharp-pointed knife or stylus and mark upon the wood lightly where the original pattern lies. Then when the antique is scraped and given two or three coats of background we may discern in a strong cross light the faint traces of our scratch line. We acquired this idea from studying Pennsylvania chests where panel outlines and many important units of a pattern are incised into the wood surface. Needless to say we cannot use this trick on decorated tinware.

RESTORING DESIGN ON A STENCILED TRAY

In the retouching or restoring of a stenciled tray the procedure is similar to the first method. We begin by cleaning judiciously with denatured alcohol to remove all white stains and too thick coatings of old shellac. Often a milky white film remains when this alcohol bath dries out, but disappears under subsequent application of a coat of clear varnish. When we have allowed this varnish twenty-four hours drying time the design reveals itself as distinctly as it ever will, and may then be traced by a crow quill pen onto our traceolene. We retrace onto stencil linen the sections of pattern which we note are missing in spots on the original tray. These stencil sections must then be cut well beyond the units we know we must supply. Extreme care must be taken, both in tracing and in cutting, that we do not deviate one fraction from the original pattern. Else our stencil when cut will not fill perfectly those damaged spaces on the tray.

Now a coat of varnish is again applied, the stencil is fitted into position and the bronze powder is delicately rubbed in when the proper moment for stenciling arrives. We must use the original tones of bronze powder that the decorator appeared to use, silver where it was silver, gold for gold, and so on.

We then have a tray with gaudy bright spots staring us in the face. On succeeding days we must work with many combinations of varnish and our transparent colors, or a tiny speck of lamp black (diluted to a transparent gray with the varnish) to tone down the glaringly new additions we have put upon the old tray. Perhaps we will have to try touching in these overtones of color several times before achieving a perfect match.

It should be said here that no retouching of a stencil pattern can be done freehand with a brush. The *texture* of stenciled bronze can never be matched except by re-stenciling as described above. But of course if such odd brush-painted bits as foliage, etc., found on stenciled trays, need retouching *these* may be touched in by a brush dipped in matching color. We must take care that this color really matches in density or transparency the original decorator's mixture. Striping may need to be completely redone on a tray thus touched up. But in this case, we have few regrets, because after all, striping is not particularly individual with any old-time designer and is just a bit of mechanical trimming.

In the end we varnish the entire tray for a more level surface, and for longer wearing qualities. If in cleaning off the old shellac, when we first began, we seemed to spoil a little of the antique tone, it will be well to return now this golden brown in our last coats of varnish.

CORRECTIVE COLOR WORKED INTO VARNISH COAT

One trick we have that might be described here is the way we occasionally work into a complete coat of flowing varnish small sections of corrective color. In leveling and setting, the varnish neatly obscures the effect of retouching. Thus oftentimes when we have made some unit a little too brilliant, so that it jumps "out of place" as part of the complete decoration, we tone it down, singly, by working in a little more umber over its too glaring countenance while applying our "antique" coats of finish varnish. This must be done *very rapidly* before the varnish has any chance to become set, and thereby to expose the places where we have done extra handling. Also, this trick works best over black backgrounds and should not be attempted upon colored grounds except by the expert decorator. We would be inclined to correct a glaring unit on a colored tray by putting a coat of varnish and dulling color over the unit itself, without overlapping onto the background.

SUPPLYING MISSING GOLD LEAF

While any touching in of missing sections on original examples is difficult, we find that repair of damaged gold leaf is enough to try our souls. For gold leaf depends upon two factors: (1) its original coloring (or alloy), and (2) its transparent overtones acquired during shellacking or varnishing. Now our gold leaf may not quite match in alloy, and our transparent overtones are bound to leave an edge by which attention to the repair is attracted. Sometimes we can escape this by regilding an entire unit, so the overtone colors will not show the edge where they leave off. But ordinarily, in spite of its disadvantages, we choose the smaller touching in, for we value the original decorator's work above our own.

RESTORING IS A SLOW PROCESS

Now that we have truly come to the last varnish coat and the final pumice and oil rub-down on our work, we might pause to reflect how many days we have had a painted antique under our hands. Allowing for bad weather days on which we cannot do varnishing and many types of design work, we have taken at least three weeks for the average restoration or reproduction. Anyone who wonders why we decorators are slow has only to try for himself! Thus we advise the decorator to carry along several pieces at different stages of completion, or he cannot make a fair investment on the time involved in his workmanship.

GOLD LEAF WASHED AWAY

Occasionally we find an old tray whereon the gold-leaf pattern must have had little protection, as it seems entirely washed away. We can see traces of there having been a pattern only by a shiny reflection of itself against the duller surface of background paint. Perhaps they laid the gold leaf in transparent gold size, without benefit of color or bronze powder for visibility. Anyhow, we recognize the fact that gold-leaf work *had* been there by the remaining etched lines, customary on gold-leaf patterns, scratched through into the background paint. If there are no badly rusted or paint-missing spots in the background of a tray like this, we may record the etched lines on our tracing paper and then re-lay gold size directly upon the traces of the original pattern. After the sizing reaches a proper stage of dryness, we lay the gold leaf and etch it according to our record.

However, if the original paint is in such a condition that it really should be removed, we proceed differently. We take japan gold size, mixed with bright gold bronze powder, and paint in a large section of the design directly upon its visible traces. Allowing this to dry, we next lay our tracing paper upon it to make an accurate record, adding thereto whatever etched lines had been used. We now may use paint remover, and strip the tray to its metal base for an entirely new start. Here again, we should call this procedure a reproduction of the original, rather than a restoration, for all traces of the old finish will have been removed.

SUPPLYING MISSING COLORS

In restoring color details missing upon old trays, we must always endeavor to separate the underlying colors from the transparent overtones by which the ultimate effect was achieved. We will find it imperative to go through an absolutely parallel build-up to arrive at a perfect match. And we will have to struggle with the difficulty always present in retouching transparent colors, where the slightest overlapping of new upon old tones attracts undue attention. Even varnish has a slight golden tone which must be reckoned with.

In trying to fill in damaged spots on a colored background tray, be sure *not* to use japan gold size as a medium, because it invariably dries darker than the original mixture. Varnish, or varnish and turpentine, will retain the exact matching of paints through the drying period.

TRAYS WITH BAD CENTER PAINT

Where a tray survives through the years with most of its border design intact, but has a badly chipped or rusted center section (undecorated), it is possible to remove the damaged paint up to the bend, where the border starts its upward turn. New paint may be filled in, the tray re-striped (as one or more stripes are generally present on a plain center tray) and the whole tray re-varnished by way of tying the whole together into a homogeneous unit. This will undoubtedly call for some transparent antique tone to be used over the new striping to "put it back" into the appearance of age. Under this procedure any seam in the paint would come at the bend in the metal edge where it quite successfully eludes detection.

However, given a tray of the "Chippendale" variety, or a rectangular tray whereon the pattern lays itself gracefully from outside edge inward toward the center, we cannot remove the center paint as far as any constructed bend in the metal tray without interfering materially with the ornamental pattern. The best procedure in this case, if time and expense be freely granted, is to start varnishing, when three or four heavy coats of varnish have been applied,[1] sandpapering may begin, with the object of removing the excess varnish from the high level of the original paint, while allowing the varnish to settle, coat by coat, in the missing or pitted sections. It may take twenty or more layers of varnish, sometimes, to approach a satisfactory surface. Some day, perhaps, we may find a material that will flow more quickly and yet be transparent enough to leave the original paint undamaged. We have tried transparent cement in *small* areas, but there is a tendency, as in glue, to crack and shrink in drying.[2]

RESTORING OIL-PAINTED CHESTS AND BOXES

Much of this chapter has been devoted to the restoring of metal trays, for the sole reason that we are most frequently called upon to rescue such articles from destruction. But the same general principles apply equally to antiques of all kinds — chairs, boxes, and smaller types of tinware, except of course, such articles as Connecticut and Pennsylvania chests, where varnishes are not considered proper. For their restoration, the student should turn to the chapter where this type of oil painting is specifically described.

CHAIRS

Chairs frequently present individual problems to the restorer. Ofttimes we find them with the original pattern more or less intact but so covered with crackled dark-toned shellac as to be badly disfigured. We may try to cut through this coating with alcohol. If we find the crust too impervious we may use fine sandpaper or steel wool, to wear away this caked gum surface gradually before an alcohol rub. If the crackle has gone through the original paint, we cannot get rid of the bare cracks but we will find that the design is much clearer after our energetic rubbing. On non-design-carrying sections of the chair we may consider the advisability of scraping down to the wood, since replacing background is not so serious an impairment in value as replacing an original decoration. When all sandpapering, alcohol rubbing and scraping have been completed, we varnish the chair and proceed with rebuilding the missing sections. Needless to say, this partial

---

[1]It will be remembered that old trays finished in asphaltum cannot be sandpapered until a thorough varnish protection has been built up to keep scratches that would be permanent from damaging the asphaltum background.

[2]Testor's cement, recently obtainable, fills well and sandpapers nicely.

filling in works more easily on dark chairs, for light backgrounds reveal the slightest variations in undercoats, overtones and surface levels.

Actual restoration, the retouching of an antique in original paint, requires so much minute individual attention that it often becomes costly. To the uninitiated it may seem unreasonable that a complete repainting job should be less expensive, but the ability to work unhampered upon broad surfaces enables the expert decorator to proceed with greater speed. Then, too, the cost of cutting particular stencils, if the article to be restored falls in this category, may have to be added to the job.

SIGNATURES

In conclusion, we might add that the restorer should place his signature upon the back of a piece or in some inconspicuous place where it will not be easily worn off. By all rights, each of us should sign our work, in order that in years to come connoisseurs may be saved the trouble of trying to determine what is what, and which decorator worked upon an antique. We should never execute our work so poorly that we are ashamed to leave our signature. We are in favor of signing a restored piece "Restored by ...."; a completely repainted piece on which the original design was definitely seen and faithfully copied should be signed, "Original design reproduced by ...."; and a piece that we have painted as we saw fit without having any clue to its original finish, might be signed simply, "Painted by ...." Inescapably, each decorator will establish his reputation for faithfully clinging to the old patterns or for failing to follow the trail of our early designs. Thus also will novice antiquarians be able to tell new work from old and be willing to absolve us from the damaging charge of faking.

PART TEN

Antiquing and Finishing

Antiquing and Finishing

W E NOW approach a highly controversial subject — the finishing of painted antiques. Many decorators believe one thing; we
believe another; and the old-timers proceeded still differently! Up
to now we have advocated absolute following of the old-timers' methods,
deviating only in the question of stencil paper. But the finish on antiques
was usually less permanent than present-day varnishes, so we must make a
choice between absolute restoration and practical durability. Besides, we
must remember that with antiques one hundred years or more have already
passed to add the softening touch of time which would not begin to mellow
our modern pigments until another century had gone by.

OLD FINISH EASILY DAMAGED

In general, most old-time painted furniture and trays were given a finish
of "spirit varnish" which is easily soluble in alcohol and which we suspect
was the equivalent of our shellac. It cracked easily; it was dark toned like
orange shellac; it turned white from heat and dampness; and all in all, it
gave little protection to the pieces on which it was used. It is the chief
reason why we present-day restorers are so often called upon to put old
trays back in condition. That this "shellac" was put on by the original
craftsman is evidenced by the way we have sometimes found this protective
coating in a wide band over the decorative design only, not over the center
of a tray where its worst qualities would be most magnified.

Over early lace-edge trays we think the decorators themselves put no
exterior finish, which may be the reason why we so seldom find their paint
in original condition. We have in mind a large lace-edge tray in perfect
state of preservation, whereon the background paint must have been
polished and re-polished, since it presents a dull finish, smooth and cool as
satin. Against this flawless background an urn and flower sprays were

painted in characteristic shades of blue, green, white and dull vermilion. There is no finish whatsoever over this tray, which is in mint condition. The old-time decorators undoubtedly knew that asphaltum, the usual finish for a lace-edge tray, never becomes bone dry and invariably causes shellac to crack when superimposed upon it.

The question is, shall we continue to use orange shellac on antique chairs, trays, etc., and no finish whatsoever on lace-edge trays, or shall we here depart from following our masters' example and give our work the protection of a good 24-hour varnish rubbed to a dull finish? The student is at liberty to make his own decision.

WE CHOOSE DULL VARNISH

Rightly or wrongly, we have made our own choice. We paint as brightly as the original decorators and give our work several coats of toned varnish to blend our glaringly new pigments into a mellow semblance of an age that is past. We chose this method for three reasons: first, because our paints, bronzes, gold leaf, etc., are absolutely as bright as when the old-time decorators used similar materials; second, because high-grade varnish preserves our work against most forms of wear and tear; third, because this method of mellow overtones enables us to produce a more vital, glowing replica of old-time work. If these three advantages more than offset the old-time use of shellac, then we have chosen rightly in adopting this procedure. After all, the early decorators would undoubtedly have preferred to use our better grade varnishes had they been universally available in their day, lest their designs be damaged by the impermanence of shellac.

The colors we use to give varnish a dull mellow tone are yellow lake, raw umber, burnt umber, with occasionally a touch of lamp black; it all depends upon which particular tone is desirable over the design we have painted. We seldom use more than two colors, usually only one, and that raw umber, which comes nearest to imparting the tone of natural age. Asphaltum is not a satisfactory "age tone" and should not be used for antiquing. Care must be taken to put very little color into each coat of varnish, as a milky effect is often apparent when too much umber is used at one time over plain black backgrounds. We must endeavor to avoid a dirty, streaky effect always present when antiquing is not kept down to the minimum in each coat of varnish. We always bear in mind, too, that when the last coat of varnish is "rubbed down" the entire antique will look duller and older.

For perfection, all particles of dust, specks of undissolved pigment or similar blemishes should be kept out of our last coat or coats of varnish. This means the use of #oo sandpaper between each coat of varnish after two have been built up over the painted pattern. The umbers, being earth colors, often possess annoying flecks in their make-up; so we try to avoid the use of these antiquing pigments in our *last* two coats of varnish. Instead of using #oo sandpaper, we frequently substitute pulverized pumice and water, rubbing carefully with the palm of our hand. Some decorators follow this up with rotten-stone and water for a greater degree of smoothness. We have even heard it said that "jeweller's rouge," used in polishing silver, may have produced the satin smooth surface on the lace-edge tray previously referred to as in mint condition. (See upper right example opposite page 148.)

LAST COAT RUB-DOWN

Our last coat of varnish is allowed to harden forty-eight hours or more. Then we rub it down with a soft cloth dipped in *crude oil*[1] and pulverized pumice. Plenty of oil is used, and rubbing must not be too vigorous or we shall get a "hazy" effect. Lemon oil is preferred to crude oil by many furniture refinishers. All trace of oil and pumice is finally removed by polishing off with a clean soft rag. We do not use pumice and water for the final rub-down, as it leaves too dull a surface. The oil rub gives the slightest suggestion of polish which is desirable. Best results are obtained if the rub-down is given in fair weather.

VARIATIONS IN TYPES OF VARNISH

A discussion of varnishes must here be in order. We prefer a 24-hour varnish that is built to stand heat and moisture, such as 24-hour Valspar. Varnish of this type requires that it be applied on a fair-weather day when the room temperature is 70° or over. Cold varnish is apt to "crawl" away from the surface to which it is applied. We do not varnish a cold tray even in a warm room; we warm the tray first. As stated previously in this book, varnish has a volatile oil which must evaporate completely within twenty-four hours. In cool or moisture-laden air, this oil partially remains and the var-

---

[1]Crude oil must not be confused with any of the linseed oils, or trouble will result. Crude oil is a dark brown fluid with a powerful oily aroma.

nished articles will have to be placed near a furnace for drying or will have to be shellacked to seal it.

In case speed is required, or bad weather has overtaken us, we may use a four-hour varnish like Super Valspar, for our finish coat or coats. In fact, we are sound believers in Super Valspar as a final coat, for two reasons — it is alcohol proof, and it rubs down nicely with pumice and crude oil. Most other alcohol-proof varnishes are difficult to rub down, and show a sort of dull "bloom" that is cloudy and disconcerting. There is a lack of cohesion between old-fashioned oil varnishes and modern synthetic varnishes which we would do well to avoid. So all in all, we approve the use of Super Valspar as an insurance against cocktail damage.

SOME OLD TRAYS WERE GLOSSY

It may seem a strange statement to make, but we feel quite certain that many trays were left glossy originally and have arrived at their present-day dullness only through having been wiped off frequently with a damp cloth. This feeling was substantiated when we acquired a tray in perfect condition that had been in storage seventy-five years! Fine Chippendale trays in untouched original paint are often very glossy. Yet the average collector today requires that his painted antiques have a pumice-and-oil rub-down.

BAD ''ANTIQUING''

We wish here to caution the new student against a pseudo-antique type of painting and artificial ageing now found on many gift shop articles. Here the background is put on heavily, showing marks where the bristles of the brush were pulled through the paint. Over this streaky surface a coat of umber or Vandyke brown is put on, and rubbed off here and there, leaving dirty clouds of brown clinging to crevices and corners. Such a method was never seen on a true antique, and we heartily resent the implication that old-time decorators smeared their workmanship in this slipshod manner.

PART ELEVEN

Painting of Furniture in Hepplewhite, Sheraton and Other Styles

Painting of Furniture in Hepplewhite, Sheraton and Other Styles

WITH the close of our American Revolution, furniture painting began its rapid rise into what was to be an extensive industry. Many who had previously been engaged in the business of coach and chaise painting turned to the decoration of furniture for household use, since demand for expensive private coaches was definitely on the wane. Chippendale, Hepplewhite and Sheraton all published design books in which the japanning of furniture was liberally suggested. In fact, the 1805 edition of Sheraton's book contains elaborate directions for the painting of chairs, and the applying of gold leaf and striping. England had famous artists like Cipriani and Angelica Kauffmann decorating elaborate furniture of the Hepplewhite and Sheraton periods. America did not produce quite such able decorators, but some of our portrait artists, such as James K. Frothingham,[1] occasionally turned to the painting of tables and other furniture.

In this country, the only Chippendale furniture that was painted seems to have been the japanned lowboys, highboys, grandfather clocks, and mirrors now generally found in museums. With the advent of Hepplewhite pieces our interest in painted chairs began, soon to be carried to unbelievable proportions in the widespread manufacture of Sheraton and Empire versions known as the "fancy chair." Then, to go with these decorated chairs, there were innumerable variations of settees, dressing tables, sewing tables, painted window cornices and bed cornices, even painted high post beds ornamented in matching gold leaf and color.

BACKGROUND PAINTS

Background paints for these pieces are mixed after the manner of coach painting, with japan colors that dry hard and fast in twenty-four hours. We take japan tube color as a base, mix with turpentine and a little varnish (or

[1] The estate of Benjamin Frothingham, Cabinetmaker of Charlestown, itemizes a bill from James K. Frothingham for the year 1828 "to painting a table — $1.50."

gold size) to a heavy cream consistency; and apply smoothly and evenly with a 1½-inch or 2-inch brush. Japan color may be toned with such artists' oil colors as are necessary to arrive at the proper shade. Very light colors are based upon the tinting of flat white paint (bought ready mixed in cans) with japan or oil colors. We also buy in cans flat black mixed to the desired consistency. But a good background paint cannot be achieved by mixing artists' oil colors with turpentine and varnish, because oil colors are mostly non-covering paints partaking in greater or less degree of transparency. Japan colors, especially mixed with the required white lead for opacity, are designed primarily for background work.

It is well to keep in mind from the very beginning just what alterations in the color will take place in applying the finish. Otherwise we might mix a shade too dark for our purposes. We must be prepared to see our dainty whites and yellows turn much yellower in finishing, for the antique varnish coats carry a yellow tone distinctly visible upon light colors. Blue must be carefully watched if we do not wish it cast on the turquoise side of the scale when it is antiqued. Of course, to aid the preserving of dull blue we may put ivory black in our antique varnish coat, instead of raw umber or burnt umber. But let us keep all these factors in mind while mixing our foundation color.

THE OLD RED

One of the most commonly used colors in the old days seems to have been Venetian red, or "Coffin's red," both unfortunately now unobtainable in japan tube colors. We arrive at an approximation of this "barn red" by mixing vermilion japan color, a little dark red (such as ascot) japan color and umber in oil, thinned down with turpentine and a little varnish or gold size. This dull red was used as a foundation coat on many Sheraton chairs and left clear, or turned into a "tortoise-shell finish" with the superimposing of thin black. The same dull red was used as a foundation coat on Hitchcock and other Empire or Victorian chairs that were given a wood grain of thin black.

NUMBER OF COATS

Single-toned backgrounds require little instruction concerning their application. Flat black and all dark colors may be limited to two coats, though more may achieve a smoother foundation. Light colors or white require three or four coats, between which a light sandpapering is advantageous.

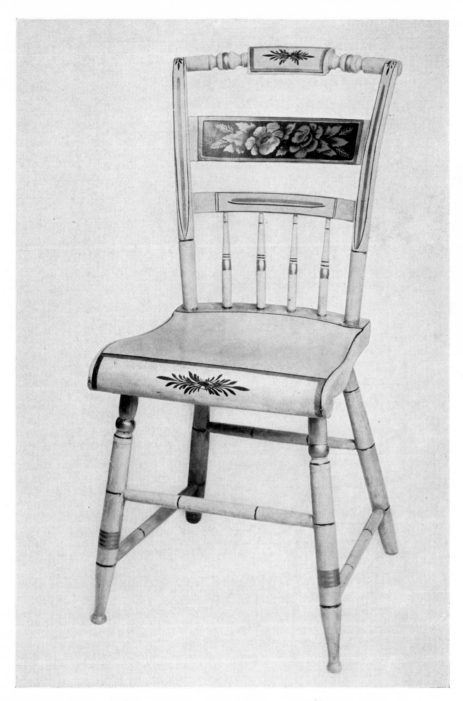

A yellow wood-seat chair, Hitchcock type, showing how the decorator made a black panel for his stenciling. Date about 1835.

A Sheraton fancy chair in pale turquoise, showing freehand bronze pattern in black and silver. Date about 1815. Courtesy of Miss Edith Rand.

Hepplewhite chair showing design (rescued from under paint) done in palest green with flowers and bird in natural colors. American, about 1785. Owned by Mrs. Harlan G. Mendenhall.

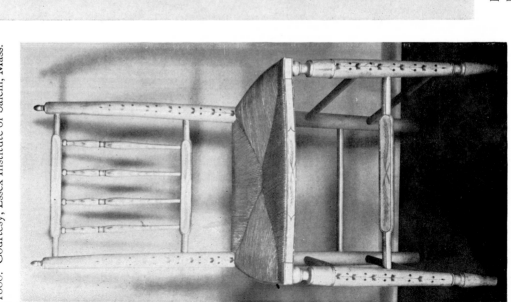

Sheraton fancy chair in yellow, decorated with green and burnt sienna pattern. Date about 1800. Courtesy, Essex Institute of Salem, Mass.

Late Boston rocker showing stenciled landscape. Date about 1840. Owned by Mrs. Louis Green.

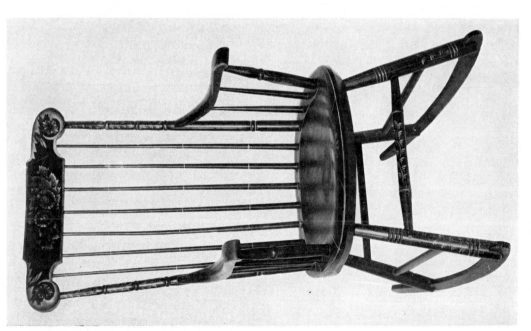

Rocking-chair labeled "Hitchcock & Alford, Hitchcocksville, Conn. Warranted." Date about 1835. Owned by the Author.

Upper left: A Southern type of chair decorated in gold leaf. Made either at Baltimore or Washington about 1825. Owned by Miss Margaret Jewell. *Upper right:* "Common yellow chair" of the 1830's. Arms are left in natural mahogany or maple finish; the seat is mottled with "putty" graining. Owned by Miss Elizabeth Stevens. *Lower left:* Pennsylvania version of the 1840's — painted in green gold and black on a salmon pink ground. Courtesy of Mrs. Richard Lenihan. *Lower right:* A very late version of stenciled chair with yellow-brown mottled seat. Date about 1850. Owned by Mrs. Richard Gordon.

We always allow twenty-four hours between coats, no matter how dry the paint may feel to our hand. Paint applied too soon will dissolve some of the previous coat and leave a disagreeable ridgy effect quite inimical to a fine surface.

TWO-TONED RED UNDER BLACK

For the two-toned red-under-black finish, we wait the required twenty-four hours and then apply flat black thinned down with turpentine. The tortoise-shell effect is pounced on with an almost dry brush in irregular fashion, leaving some sections quite red and others quite black in the mottling. A grained effect in the black was far more usual. In this case the wood grain may be achieved by pressure on the brush with which we apply the black. A more pronounced grain is achieved by pulling a crumpled stiff cloth across the slat immediately upon applying the thin black paint. A crumpled piece of newspaper may be used; crushed cellophane; a piece of cardboard cut in irregular notches; a broad piece of cork; a notched piece of strawberry-basket wood, or in fact anything you may think of to gain the desired effect. Sometimes they had an old and stiffened paint brush out of which hairs had been cut in irregular fashion. Evidence exists in the chair-painting shop at the museum in Doylestown, Pennsylvania, that they even made use of a stencil to apply a grained black finish.

RED OVER BLACK

In a few rare cases, they grained chairs in red over black with fine irregular lines. Many early chairs from Lambert Hitchcock's factory were so grained with a masterly bit of artistry. It appears that a sort of "piped grainer" must have been contrived from fastening a group of fine brushes together, one after another like a section of board fence. Trying to match this sort of graining almost defies the patience of a saint.

TWO-TONED BROWN

A different sort of two-toned finish, found primarily on painted chairs, is the brown "rosewood" or "walnut" finish. Here a thin black grain was applied directly to the bare wood, sometimes painted in freehand, sometimes with the group of smaller brushes fastened into a grainer as just described. According to some directions found in an old book, this graining was frequently done with a strong acid which burned into the wood. If, in cleaning off an old chair which once possessed this type of graining, we take care not to mar the wood surface, most of this grain will remain in the wood and can be preserved. After the fine black graining is applied, we wait twenty-four hours and then varnish the chair with a coat of dull brown, achieved by mixing various combinations of raw umber, umber, burnt sienna and black with varnish to get the shade we desire. Some Sheraton Empire chairs (those with round fronts), and elaborate Hitchcock chairs with pierced slats, are finished in this two-toned brown background. Much gold leaf is generally found in their superimposed decorative design work.

BLACK GROUND FOR ELABORATE DESIGN

In painting the backgrounds of Hitchcock chairs, and many Boston rockers whose finish coincided, the whole chair was grained except for the front face of the main design-carrying slat. Here the chair received two coats of heavy flat black paint instead of the red-under-black groundwork. We suppose that the early decorators believed the graining would detract from the effectiveness of their design. This solid black facing was also used on those two-toned brown finished Hitchcocks which had pierced cornucopia or eagle-shaped center slats. In the case of the Lambert Hitchcock chairs which received the rarer red over-graining of fine lines, this distraction was left off the main design slat, or slats (if two of them were elaborately decorated). Yet the upright posts, front of seat frame, and other decorated sections, were grained to match the rest of the chair.

LATE STYLE CHAIRS GRAINED

Late Boston rockers, and late style fiddle-back cane-seat chairs, however, often had the pronounced painted grain running through under the main pattern, much to the detriment of its effectiveness. Stenciling placed upon a strongly grained background cannot call upon that illusive quality of darkness inherent in straight black, that is the very making of bronze stenciled beauty.

PAINTING OF SEATS

While we are on the subject of Hitchcocks, and rush- or cane-seat chairs, it might be in place here to say that the painting of seats was advocated in Sheraton's book, where he calls it a strong preservative. Thus we find many of our Sheraton fancy chairs were painted a soft straw color or oyster white on the rush-seat section. We of today have been accustomed to seeing rush seats left natural, but in the heyday of painted Sheratons it must have been more customary to paint them. Again, on a labeled cane-seat Hitchcock chair in original paint, we have seen evidences of painting the cane black. While another with the same label seems never to have had the cane except in natural finish. So we may draw the conclusion that in later days it was all a matter of individual choice, or of labor saving during rapid factory production. It is not advisable to try to remove paint from rush or cane seats once it has been applied. Paint remover weakens the seat fibres and a scraper used on them would succeed mostly in breaking the strands. It is far better to repaint the seats in some desirable color awaiting the time when the seat finally gives out and has to be replaced.

Needless to say, we are not advocating the painting of rush or cane on such chairs as were never made *to be decorated*. Early slat-back chairs and bannister backs might have had an original plain paint finish but they were almost never decorated, and so should have unpainted rush or cane.

YELLOW-BROWN GRAINING

A curious two-toned effect frequently found on black or yellow wood-seat chairs is a mottled brown called "vinegar painting," or "putty graining." The foundation coats were a soft yellow, then a variegated brown made by mixing burnt umber in vinegar was applied to the seat, with patches of raw umber and burnt umber worked in here and there. Next a roll of putty the size of a thumb was taken as a tool to work patterns into the brown vinegar coating. Linseed oil in the putty would cause the brown glaze to separate in curious seaweed-like effect. The putty roll would be placed repeatedly at regular intervals to form a sort of border pattern, or it would be wheeled around in circle formation to form fans and similar whorled figures.

SMOKED GROUND

Another strange two-toned effect found on chairs and small objects like boxes and bellows, was the "marbled" or smoked finish. Hard as it is to believe, a candle was really used to do the smoking. It was generally applied over a flat white background. If sizing was used to fix the smoking, it was allowed to reach that almost dry stage when stenciling would be in order.

Then a lighted candle was passed rapidly under the surface of the chair or bellows, taking care not to scorch or blister the foundation painting. A subsequent coat of varnish or gold size was used as a fixative in cases where the smoking had been done against the plain white paint.

MIX PAINT IN TIGHTLY COVERED CONTAINER

But let us return once more to our mixing of background colors for chair painting. It is well to mix them in a tightly covered tin or jar so that some may be kept for trimming, in case there are errors that have to be painted out, or in case the chair is inadvertently bumped before finishing. If a skin forms on the paint after standing, we remove it as intact as possible by running a tool around the edge where the skin joins the inner wall of our container, and then lifting out the skin. On no account do we allow this toughened paint to be mixed in with the fluid paint, for it will form disastrous lumps in our paint surface. If the skin is not tough enough to be lifted, then we must resort to straining our paint through several layers of cheesecloth or a very fine mesh wire strainer.

SELECTION OF DECORATIVE DESIGN

When our background colors have been duly applied and the last coat is 24 hours dry, we may decide upon the decorative design with which we are going to proceed. Great care should be exercised in this selection in order that we may produce a satisfying result. First of all, we must have at hand records of original designs of the proper period, unless of course we are lucky enough to have found traces of *the original* design still clinging to our piece. Hepplewhite chairs have patterns with pink roses, blue forget-me-nots, classical urns and small birds predominating, much in the manner of lace-edge tray patterns that probably coincide in date. These designs are largely in natural colors, though we have seen one or two examples where the pattern was heavily weighted with gold leaf. Sheraton fancy chairs were daintily adorned with classic designs of gold leaf, color or freehand bronze. There appears to have been no end of ingenuity in this period of good taste. The decorator called upon all emblems of classic origin — the lyre, the cornucopia, the husk flower, the bow and quiver of arrows, the drapery swag and tassel, the acanthus leaf, the ivy leaf, grapes and grape leaves, laurel wreaths, rosettes, festoons of dainty flowers, even the great god Neptune and his sea horse! Early Sheraton fancy chairs have the almost square rush seat where the frontal section shows just the faintest of outward bows. Later Sheratons, from 1815 to 1820, as nearly as we can ascertain, adopted the round front seat frame, the widened top slat and consequent emboldening of decorative pattern. Then the so-called Hitchcock chair began to appear with its straight front seat frame protected and adorned by a semi-round turned bar. The best chairs of the Hitchcock variety boasted of gold leaf on their turnings and on the conventionalized patterns that ornamented the seat frame, stiles and hand-grip sections. If the center slat was pierced, or shaped in cornucopia form, such gold leaf was sure to be present. The fruits in the rich gold cornucopia would likely be stenciled in pale-colored bronze powder, by way of contrast. Other more ordinary versions of Hitchcock chairs were simply stenciled with bowls of fruit, bunches of grapes, assorted flowers, fruits and leaves, in bronze powders ranging from silver through pale gold to deep gold and fire color. About 1840 there appeared a predilection for stenciled bronze landscapes on Hitchcock type chairs, Boston rockers and late Empire "fiddle-back" chairs, though some still persisted in flower and fruit patterns.

WOOD-SEAT CHAIRS AND ROCKERS

Along side of rush- and cane-seat "fancy chairs" there grew up the wood-seat chair which was primarily a Windsor, but which went through so many variations as time progressed that it merged into a complex hybrid. In fact, there are times when we can hardly call the wood-seat chair a Windsor at all so closely has it become a counterpart of Sheraton or Hitchcock chairs. Windsors, even in the beginning, were painted chairs due to the fact that three kinds of wood were used in their construction. But the only ornament in the early days was a contrastingly colored stripe. Then as the Sheraton fancy chair became popular we find the wood-seat Windsor broadening its top slat a little into what is known as the "step-down," "fan-back," or "comb-back" Windsor, with a very simple version of a Sheraton pattern on its top slat. These designs were often just brush-stroke patterns executed in the contrasting stripe color. Next we find a version of wood-seat chair with a straight broad top slat, only four or five upright spindles between the side posts, and legs that had either Sheraton or "bamboo" turnings. These were generally embellished with gold leaf, or freehand bronze patterns, similar to their rush-seat contemporaries. Later varieties had bronze stencil patterns suggestive of those found on Hitchcock-type chairs.

Then there were the high-backed Windsor rockers with broad top slat decorated in Sheraton classic style. These chairs were soon (1825) to adopt the roll-front seat, the rolling arm, and rounded-end top slat to become the true Boston rocker of tremendous popularity. Stencil patterns were usual on the Bostons, for they coincided with that period of factory production and cut-throat competition which lasted from 1825 to 1870. Victorian chairs with their curving top slat and daintily turned spindles reverted to the early idea of flowers in natural colors, pink and white roses, blue daisies, yellow brown-eyed Susans and chaste white lilies of the valley. Thus we see the fashion of decoration swinging once around the circle in nearly a century from the days of painted Hepplewhite in natural colors.

COLLECTING DESIGNS

Obviously, to be sure of the correct patterns for each of these periods, we should gather many records of authentic original designs. We have discarded pencil and crayon sketches as inadequate, and now make completely painted tracings of a pattern, whenever possible. Then the subtleties which consist of density in paint, or transparency, can be accurately recorded, and the exact shades can be matched far better than by crayon. Many collectors and antique dealers are quite willing to allow their pieces to be copied, knowing full well that there can be only one original and its value cannot be detracted from.

Once the pattern is decided upon, we proceed to apply it by the methods described in earlier chapters of this book. Next we stripe or band our piece, and complete all corrections and bits of trimming. For this final perfecting we use some of our background paint which we have preserved in a screw-top jar. Last of all, we apply the final coats of antique-toned varnish according to the directions in the chapter on finishing. When we are done, our furniture should look like old pieces in excellent state of paint preservation, not like newly re-decorated examples.

PART TWELVE

Oil-Painted Boxes and Chests

Oil-Painted Boxes and Chests

IT HAS been generally believed by antiquarians that early chests made in rural sections of New England, New York and Pennsylvania were not decorated by the foregoing varnish methods. Indeed, they look with distress upon a chest that some well-meaning person has thought to rejuvenate by a coat of dull varnish. Now, we agree that Pennsylvania chests and Taunton chests should be painted by slow oil methods, but, frankly, we are on the fence about Connecticut chests. Ever since reading in the inventory of Mr. Benjamin Beech, who died at Durham, Connecticut, in the year 1712, "One varnish cuberd" valued at 2£:10 shillings, we are inclined to believe that varnish was on the *outside of that cupboard!* Why? To protect the decorative painting. The town of Durham was in that well-known section of Connecticut near Guilford where decorated chests and cupboards were made. And in the inventory of Charles Gillam, a carpenter or joiner of Saybrook (the adjoining town to Guilford) we find an item of "colours, brushes, boxes and gums"! — gums were the basis for varnish, and here, we believe, is the maker and decorator of certain "Guilford" chests.

So we dispute the theory that Connecticut chests should not be varnished, but concede the point that Pennsylvania and Massachusetts rural chests certainly were done with linseed oil and turpentine, and we allow any antiquarian wishing to be on the safe side of the controversy to have his Connecticut chests restored by oil methods, for varnish cannot be easily removed once it has been applied, yet it can be added on top of oil painting at any time.

OIL FINISH NEEDS OILING ONCE A YEAR

Pieces decorated with this slow oil process come eventually to have a dull effect as the oil "strikes in" and leaves the pigments with a sort of "bloom" upon them. Eventually these paints will lose their vitality and come to a "powdering" stage when they show wear, and begin to flake away almost imperceptibly. Therefore, such chests should be given a thorough oiling at least once a year, to keep vitality in the paint. A soft cloth and raw linseed oil is all that is needed. At first the chest will appear dark, as if varnished, but in the course of two or three weeks, the oil will begin to "strike in" again to the thirsty wood-fibres, and the chest painting will settle down to its previous soft coloring. If the chest has appeared dirty, a light washing twenty-four hours prior to the oiling may be judiciously attempted, and after the oil has been applied we try to keep dust and dirt from settling in its vicinity. This may be accomplished by blocking up two card tables to the required height so that a protective dust sheet may be draped without touching the newly oiled chest at any point.

RESTORING OIL-PAINTED CHESTS

In restoring an old chest on which the original decoration is in fairly good condition, we proceed in a method similar to that just described, namely, cleaning with soap and water (or carefully applied alcohol if necessary), and then a thorough oiling. After waiting at least a week for this oil to oxidize and harden, we proceed to mix matching japan and oil colors with raw linseed oil, a small quantity of turpentine, and a few drops of japan gold size to speed up the drying just a little. Paints so mixed may be used to supply missing sections of background color. Then after two weeks, missing sections of design work may be filled in similarly, keeping in mind the fact that where two newly applied oil paints touch each other there will be a strong tendency for them to "spread" or run into each other. It is well to wait a week between contiguous or superimposed colors, in order that this spreading may be avoided. Now the chest is allowed to stand for two, three, or four weeks to "harden" before the antiquing is applied.

ANTIQUING OIL-PAINTED FINISH

On these chests, where varnish is not to be used, our antiquing consists of raw linseed oil with a little turpentine, a few drops of japan gold size, and raw umber oil color. This we rub on with a soft clean cloth, free of lint, stroking the full length of the chest from end to end in even parallel lines. We allow this to dry from two to three weeks before repeating, until the desired mellow tone of age is acquired.

If we wish to start from scratch, with an old chest, we take care to remove all traces of surface paint with remover and steel wool, followed by a careful wiping with turpentine or carbona. If old "Coffin's red" was used, and some of the color has sunk into the wood as a stain, we do not need to worry, for our paints will cover. Next we chalk in all our panel outlines, measuring carefully. We find it advisable to judge this panel layout critically from across the room, that we may be certain all units are properly balanced and evenly spaced. If we are doing a Taunton or Connecticut type design not based on panels, we chalk in the distribution of main stem lines to see that the curves are pleasingly disposed. After *final* corrections have been made, we follow the important lines with a sharp-pointed instrument. In this way we have a guiding line discernible when background paints have been applied.

An oil-painted chest seldom requires more than two coats of background paint. Old chests, it will be observed, often show the wood grain as if there had been little paint used. Strangely enough, on Pennsylvania chests, we have seen frequent evidence that the ivory-white panel grounds were painted first with the chest background swung around them to avoid contact! Inch-wide borders around the panels covered all irregularities where panel left off and background overlapped. Sometimes, it has occurred to us, the custom of deeply scratching a panel outline was cleverly designed to stop the creeping of background paint into the panel color.

TWO-TONED BACKGROUND

Not all early chests had a single-toned background. Some were mottled with white and dull red "sponging" on a dark brownish-black background. Some were given a "combed" graining in black on natural wood. Pennsylvania chests frequently had two-toned backgrounds, with swirls worked into the mottling by clever twists of a cloth, a brush or a finger. Some two-toned Pennsylvania chests had the overtone consisting of raw linseed oil and one of the partially transparent colors, into which a figure was subsequently worked with a two-inch brush dipped in clear turpentine. Drops of turpentine worked upon the oil color and made it separate in curious seaweed-like figures. Some chests were painted cream white and then given a putty graining in a sort of geometric layout, or a cloth graining in strange bold swirls. Old-time variations tax our ingenuity to match, and defy our vocabulary to describe! All we can do is experiment until we come upon a combination that will produce the effects we see on old examples.

OTHER BACKGROUND COLORS

Connecticut chests have been observed with brown, black, dull red, and dark green backgrounds, against which patterns in white stand out strikingly. Taunton chests were brown-black in coloring,[1] with the possible exception of one that might have been a soft French blue. Another Taunton chest, seemingly experimental, was brown-black all except the drawer front where black trees were drawn against a dull red-brown ground work. Some early chests from Connecticut, Massachusetts and New Hampshire, were sparingly decorated on the wood, as though paints were difficult to obtain and expensive.

Not so the Pennsylvania dower chests, for here paints were used boldly and lavishly in patterns of peasant flavor. Customary background colors were dull red, two-toned brown, sea green, dark green or blue (both medium and very dark tones being frequent). Almost invariably the feet were painted black and the moulding just above the base, as well as the moulding around the lid, was given a color contrasting to the general background paint. Panel borders generally reflected a color prominent in the decorative design work on the panel. With all due respect to other writers, we would say most emphatically, that Pennsylvania chests never had black backgrounds.

DESIGN PAINTS

The design colors are mixed similarly with raw linseed oil, and a few drops of japan gold size. We find that oil has a tendency to make even japan tube colors appear a bit transparent. This is as it should be, for old examples also display this soft transparency. On Connecticut and Taunton chests, the entire decorative design was frequently based on white, with overtones of color touched in on leaves and flowers. Other times, white was mixed *in* a color to make it hold its own against a dark background. For we must remember that many of the early colors were either transparent or partook of transparency, like Prussian blue, verdigris, yellow ochre and

[1]One or two Taunton chests have been found to have a background paint that is water solvent.

all the brown earth colors. Vermilion was one of the few really opaque colors of early days.

In applying decorative design colors according to this oil method, we must take care to put them on sparingly, as they are apt to drip or run while in a vertical position. To eliminate this danger many of the old-time designers mixed their decorative paints quite thickly and allowed them a long while to dry. Of course *they* were not waiting around impatiently to put on antique coats as we are, and were therefore at liberty to take all the time they wanted.

Since the old-time country decorator did not confine all his efforts to the painting of chests, what we have said about mixing paints applied equally well to other products turned out by the same sort of craftsman. He found winter occupation, no doubt, fashioning salt boxes, bible boxes, trinket boxes, and the like, with simple or elaborate designs according to his fancy. But in decorating them, he would have clung to the same slow oil painting methods he had long been accustomed to use. So also should we cling to this more tedious method if we aim to restore or reproduce his handiwork faithfully.

PART THIRTEEN

General Directions for the Painting of Tinware

General Directions for the Painting of Tinware

T HE old-time painting of tinware was of two kinds — the unbaked, which resembled in method the painting of furniture just described, and the baked variety where a large proportion of varnish was used and the articles were fired in ovens to a hard and enduring surface. We individual craftsmen of today can hardly hope to reproduce this latter work, unless we want to go in for the expense of kilns and quantity production. Still, if we wish, we can have our pieces "japanned" by commercial japanners who may be located in a number of larger cities like Boston, New York, Philadelphia, etc. We will experience difficulty, however, in obtaining any subtle variations in color that we may be seeking, and we will regret that japanners do not produce that flat paint finish which facilitates the laying of gold-leaf patterns.

So we may turn our attention to the home painting of backgrounds, with an easy conscience, knowing full well that our early tinsmiths working in their small shops must have followed a similar procedure. For the tinworkers soon learned that tin finish on iron was not proof against rust, and that paints and varnishes added enduring qualities and attractive appearances to their handiwork.

PREPARATION OF BACKGROUNDS

In starting out to paint an old tray, for instance, it is necessary to remove all vestiges of paint before beginning our new finish. This is comparatively simple by employing paint remover and steel wool, or a steel scraper. If the tin surface is pitted badly with rust, a rust killer should be used. There is an acid called "Rusticide," procurable at automobile accessory stores, that attacks rust and is supposed to prevent its return. Rusticide is applied and allowed to stand for several minutes, then the rusty surface is scrubbed with steel wool, wire brushes, or any strong abrasive. Afterward, we must clean away the greasy residue by wiping with strong soap and water, or carbon tetrachloride. Otherwise, paints have a tendency to pick up the oily residue of Rusticide, and fail to dry out properly. After all possible rust is removed, we build up the surface by using a "metal primer" followed by several coats of flat black paint (or a color) twenty-four hours being allowed between each coat, and a light sandpapering between the last two or three coats. We have always found it wise to paint badly pitted or rusted trays black, as the dark surface is most helpful in concealing the irregularity of surface. Those who wish to take the trouble, can build a perfection finish by laying 6 or 7 coats well rubbed with #oo sandpaper between. Metal primer is a heavy bodied paint, somewhat sandy in texture, that fills our crevices quite rapidly. It is desirable upon brand new tinware, as it clings tenaciously to the shiny surface. On the other hand, we can roughen the new tin surface with fine sandpaper or steel wool, and then apply our flat black paint mixed with a little varnish so that it will cling to the metal. (Or we may use a japan color paint, also mixed with a good proportion of varnish.) On a smooth foundation, it is possible to "get by" with only two coats of flat black paint, providing these are evenly applied. *But,* two coats make the absolutely irreducible minimum, in black or any opaque color.

When mixing background colors for tinware we may follow the directions for furniture painting if we wish a flat finish paint for gold-leaf work. This means that we take japan tube colors as a base, combined with oil color, if necessary to obtain certain shades, and mix with turpentine and a very little varnish to heavy cream consistency. Or we may follow the old-time custom of mixing our japan coach colors largely with varnish to make a glossy finish. "Handmaid of the Arts"[1] tells us, surprisingly, that most japanning colors were mixed with "spirit varnish" which seems to be shellac. Varnish should be smoother and far more durable, however. Two or three coats of medium or dark colors may suffice, but more, sandpapering between, will always add to the perfection of finish. We never try to work upon a specked background, where dust or particles of paint seem to be imbedded. These specks will become magnified to our mortification when we apply our antique finish. So, all possible care taken *in the beginning* with our foundation coats, will be well rewarded in the end.

[1]Published in London, 1758.

Only the experienced decorator should try to paint a white or light-toned tray. Flat white paint, bought ready mixed in cans, may be used for the white. It can be toned to an ivory, if desired, by adding a bit of yellow ochre and raw umber, but remember that antique varnish coats will accomplish the same result. Light tints of other colors may be obtained by similarly mixing a little japan or oil color with the flat white. We always save some of these mixed colors until our piece is finished, as it may be needed in painting out errors, or in trimming that bad-actor gold leaf if it is used in our design work. On light-colored backgrounds, it is difficult to make erasures, so the decorator should endeavor to work with great accuracy. One thing might help, however, and that is painting the background and allowing it to harden for a month or longer before starting the design work. If this is done, then erasures in the pattern will be less likely to mar the background surface (the older a paint is, the less it dissolves under contact with carbona). Light-colored backgrounds should have at least three coats, and preferably more for perfect coverage.

PAINTING BACK FIRST

In applying paints to a tin tray, for instance, start with the tray turned face down, and paint the raised border section. Then slip the tray over, and paint the regular surface, beginning first with the raised border and ending with the field, or "floor" of the tray. Strokes should extend the entire length of the surface they cover. No short, choppy strokes are allowable. The very back of the tray, which comes in contact with the table, we like to leave unscraped and unpainted if it is an antique, by way of proof. But when this section is to be painted, it is given two coats of black after everything else is finished. Even on white and colored trays this section was painted black in the old days.

ASPHALTUM OR SHINY BROWN GROUNDS

Many small and odd articles of Early American tinware, such as tea caddies, bread baskets, trinket boxes and the like, were given a background of asphaltum over the bright tin. This is that peculiarly shining brown, or brown-black that is impossible to match with any other pigment. Asphaltum comes in tube form, or mixed with varnish in cans, and is nothing more nor less than a refined form of asphalt. It is a peculiar substance, in that it is never perfectly dry, according to the chemists, although it seems dry to all intents and purposes. It is one of the finishes that became particularly durable after firing. But we can handle it at home today if we keep in mind its bad habit of attracting gold leaf on the slightest provocation.

Asphaltum may be made to run all the way down the scale from a pale golden brown background color, to a deep rich brown that borders on black. It all depends upon how much varnish is used in toning the asphaltum base, by which it is applied. Any of the *transparent* paints may be incorporated in the mixture, particularly yellow lake for the golden brown, and alizarin crimson for the red-brown shade we sometimes encounter. Two coats of asphaltum, as it comes ready mixed in the can, will make a heavy brown that is almost black. It must be spread on carefully and quickly, with methodical strokes, and no more rehandling by the brush than is absolutely necessary. Asphaltum backgrounds, as we see from old examples, were frequently streaky in appearance because of its tendency to show brush handling, and to run down a vertical or slanting surface. It therefore behooves us to use the brush fairly dry and not too heavily charged.

OTHER TRANSPARENT GROUND COLORS

Other transparent backgrounds were applied over new tin to achieve a clear and shining color. We may match them today by adding our transparent alizarin crimson, yellow lake, verdigris, Prussian blue and raw umber to varnish in whatever combinations we may desire. If the tin is no longer bright, the effect will be disappointing; but we may simulate bright tin by laying true silver powder upon the background before starting our colored varnishes.

CRYSTALLIZED AND GRAINED BACKGROUNDS

Still further use of transparent background colors was made in achieving what was called "marbled" or "crystallized" tin. Three different recipes for this finish are described in old books, all calling for the use of strong acids. The resultant effect looks very much like modern galvanized iron. But, due to the fact that these acids were strong, the tin is often worn through and in poor condition today. Once the "silver" surface of tin has turned dull and leaden, we cannot succeed in crystallizing it. If we must re-do such a piece in this manner, then we will need to have it re-tinned first.

Muriatic acid or Rusticide (which may consist largely of this acid) may be applied to the bright tin with an old brush or a piece of cotton. We will have little control over the crystal effect that will appear of its own accord. Afterwards, we should wash the tin thoroughly and allow at least twenty-four hours drying time before varnishing with the desired asphaltum or transparent color. Some painted tin articles have a sort of grained background applied in thin flat black paint diluted with turpentine. The process really does not differ from what we do on Hitchcock chairs. We may use whatever tool will achieve the "figure" prominent in the grain. Some of these tin pieces were grained first, directly, against the bright tin, and then "lacquered" over with thin asphaltum, or alizarin-crimson-tinted varnish.

LACE-EDGE TRAYS AND TORTOISE SHELL GROUNDS

Lace-edge trays, "gallery" trays and important painted articles belonging to their early period, often had a strange build-up. A first coat of flat black paint or very dull dark asphaltum was applied, with irregular patches of silver leaf laid at odd intervals. Asphaltum, a varnish substance, could be made to receive these patches when it was almost dry. After twenty-four hours, a coat of fiery bright alizarin crimson was laid on in varnish. Twenty-four hours later still, a coat of dark asphaltum was laid on and immediately, with a crumpled cloth, high lights over the silver patches were "lifted" out. This procedure is briefly mentioned in the 1688 book on japanning, and is carried on today by the best of decorators.

There was a variant of this "tortoise-shell" finish, wherein no silver leaf was used, but patches of red lead or vermilion were substituted. These were not, of course, transparent, and the layer of alizarin crimson was omitted. But the final coat of asphaltum was allowed to reveal the underlying vermilion in cloud effects similar to the above-mentioned method.

If we are in a hurry, however, we may give lace-edge trays the equally authentic but far less interesting finish of two-coat asphaltum, or two-coat flat black paint.

BRONZE BACKGROUNDS

A distinctive background finish found primarily on pie-crust trays, but occasionally on rectangular trays, wooden trinket boxes, small card cases, etc., is the shaded bronze background. Foundation coats of flat black are built up, smoothly polished to the nth degree. Then a coat of 24-hour varnish is laid on and allowed to reach that stage of *almost* dryness which is used in bronze stenciling and in gold-leaf work. Then a group of bronze powders ranging from pale gold through deeper golds to copper and dark brown is selected. Charging our stenciling velvet with these powders, we lay on a large cloud of bronze that is a clear shining pale gold at the center, and is graduated into deep-toned chocolate brown at the outer edges. The thinly used brown is allowed to disappear into nothingness as it approaches our black background. Where a bold bunch of flowers was painted near the centerbase of such a tray, we often observe the gold-bronze fading away rapidly behind the flower position, in order that lower leaves and stems may appear painted in green against a black ground. As a precautionary measure, it is well to varnish a shaded bronze background when it is twenty-four hours old, that erasures may be permitted during our design application.

INSIDE OF TIN BOXES

It is customary to leave the inside of the country tin boxes in bright metal, unpainted. But occasionally we feel the necessity of painting the interior of a box that is now badly rusted or stained. Such internal painting should be applied with a small brush stroke evenly from corner to corner, the whole completed before attempting any exterior painting. The reason for this will be obvious when we find how easily paint spills over the edges and drips down behind the hinges. We leave the box wide open while this inside paint is drying.

DECORATION AND FINISHING

Once the background paint is applied, our procedure is similar to that outlined under the painting of furniture, namely, selecting a design of the proper type and period, applying it by the methods described in earlier sections of this study, and then finishing with several coats of brown-toned varnish. On trays, it is most desirable that we remember to use alcohol-proof varnish for the last coats. Otherwise we might have to restore our own reproduction, which would reflect discredit on our workmanship.

Now that the restoring of antique trays is becoming such a hobby, it might be well to describe here the different types of patterns usually found on various shapes of trays. Since shape cannot be shifted it unavoidably dictates the kind of decorative design work which will look as though it "belonged."

First of all, we believe, there were the lace-edge trays, round, oval and rectangular, the latter sometimes being equipped with ornamental "Chippendale" brass handles. The painting on these trays had a Rembrandtesque quality, in that the design seems to come up out of a dim background to distinct high lights of great interest. Parts of the leaves, stems, flowers and fruit seem to be in deep shadow. Many of the pigments were transparent in those days, making themselves visible mostly when mixed with white, "King's yellow," or vermilion. The high lights of a lace-edge tray decoration "carried" the pattern into reality. Designs generally consisted of full-blown or bud roses; tiny daisy-like flowers in blue, cream white and dull vermilion; amaryllis, tulips, narcissi, morning glories, or a collection of fruits with peaches, pears and strawberries predominating. Sometimes a bird perched nonchalantly amid the fruit or flowers. Sometimes an Adam's urn draped with a blue swag formed the central feature. A delicate gold-leaf border ran around the outside edge of the tray, just where the pierced rim begins to take its rise. Also the outermost scalloped edge beyond the piercing was generally gilded to complete the "framing" of the pattern. Then there were unpierced versions of the round and oval trays, which may have been put on the market as a less expensive product. These unpierced trays received painting identical in workmanship with their more elaborate relatives. A cross section of such a tray would show the rim following identical curves, viz. — (‿_____‿).

GALLERY TRAYS

Closely related were the "gallery" trays where the edge rose deeply slanted (_____/) or absolutely perpendicular (|_____|) to the field of the tray. Many of these were decorated in identical manner with lace-edge trays, particularly those which were pierced with a vertical slot, or "keyhole"-shaped cut. The unpierced gallery-edge tray, oval in shape, often received elaborate landscapes, which may be attributed to fine artists. Others had an oval center portrait of a lady in Gainsborough style, beautifully subdued in color. Borders on these trays were generally in elaborate gold leaf, with minute touches of white or color. Some of these oval medallion trays were done upon an intricately striped background difficult to describe. Parallel lines in alternating colors seem to have been ruled on with a ruling pen, for the lines are mechanically perfect and unvarying.

There were also oval gallery trays with gold-leaf center patterns in classic style combined with gold-leaf borders. Then there were many oval trays with nothing but an elaborate gold-leaf border design, and plain black or color center, relieved with a simple stripe or tiny running vine. In general, we place the gallery-edge tray in the Hepplewhite and Sheraton periods from 1780 to 1810.

DEEP-EDGED OCTAGONALS

Octagonal trays with massive outward flaring edges seem to have crept into existence during the classic Hepplewhite period and to have persisted until stenciled rectangular trays came into full swing. Therefore, early octagonal trays had classic gold-leaf designs with swags of drapery, rosettes, sunbursts, and running borders of thistle, rose, tulip, forget-me-not, grape or acanthus-leaf motifs. Later octagonal trays exhibited early bronze stenciled borders where many freehand details are painted in. Some of these had central landscape medallions simply executed in natural colors.

RECTANGULAR TRAYS

Just when the rectangular tray with curving corners first came into being it is difficult to say, as it was popular over a long period of time. Once, in our travels, we saw a rectangular lace-edge tray with brass handles, that had curving corners instead of diagonally-mitred square corners. This would lead us to believe that the rectangular tray with rounding corners was just developing at the end of the lace-edge tray period. But this evidence is by no means conclusive. The most intricate and painstaking painted designs appear to be on those rectangular curved-corner trays which have a horizontal border about 1½ inches wide.[1] A cross section of these trays would look like this (⌐___⌐). We are inclined to date the earliest of such trays around 1760 or 1770, for the design work is so intricate as to be prohibitive in cost. It resembles the work of men who did the extremely elaborate japanning of highboys and mirrors, and in consequence, died insolvent. Much tiny pen work in gold is apparent in these designs, flowers are toned in floating color, and leaves show masterly high lights in freehand bronze work. By far the most frequently encountered form of metal tray is the rectangular curved-corner tray with 2½- to 3-inch border curving upward and outward, over a heavy wire rim. (Poor examples sometimes omitted the

[1]Horizontal border specimens were called "Sandwich Trays" by the old-time japanners.

LACE-EDGE AND OVAL GALLERY TRAYS

Upper left: Unpierced tray of lace-edge period — about 1780. Owned by Mrs. Arthur Oldham. *Upper right:* Large lace-edge tray, either English or American made. Possibly attributable to Paul Revere's tin shop, about 1785. Owned by the Author. *Center:* Oval gallery tray showing red-coated officer gazing upon an allegorical representation of Washington's tomb. Date 1800. Possibly painted in England for American trade. Owned by the Author. *Lower left:* Oval gallery tray with "keyhole" piercing. Design work similar to lace-edge trays. Date 1780 to 1800. Owned by the Author. *Lower right:* Oval gallery tray with design in gold leaf and white. Date about 1800. Owned by Miss Louise Coburn.

FOUR EXAMPLES OF OCTAGONAL TRAYS

Upper left: An early version showing lace-edge-tray-type painting. Date 1780. Owned by Mrs. Frank H. Stevens, Jr. *Upper right:* Heavy-edge tray, possibly English made. Date about 1800. Owned by Mrs. Thorndike Endicott. *Lower left:* Country tin tray made by Zachariah Stevens, Portland, Me., about 1805. Owned by Mrs. Robert Stone. *Lower right:* Country tin tray with seam in center. Date about 1825. Owned by Mrs. Charles S. Draper.

FIVE EXAMPLES OF RECTANGULAR TRAYS

Upper left: A tray with horizontal edge called "Sandwich." Very intricate decoration in free-hand bronze and gold leaf. Date about 1770. Owned by Mrs. Warren K. Lewis. *Upper right:* A freehand bronze border on silver-leaf band ground under paint. About 1800. Owned by Mrs. Arthur Oldham. *Center:* Running gold-leaf border. (Demonstrated on Pages 234 and 235.) Date about 1800. Courtesy of Mrs. Irving W. Bailey. *Lower left:* Tray with gold-leaf border; center painted in color characteristic of the 1830's. Owned by the Author. *Lower right:* Elaborately stenciled tray of a type that seems to have been made in Maine about 1830. Owned by Mrs. Charles Foster Brown.

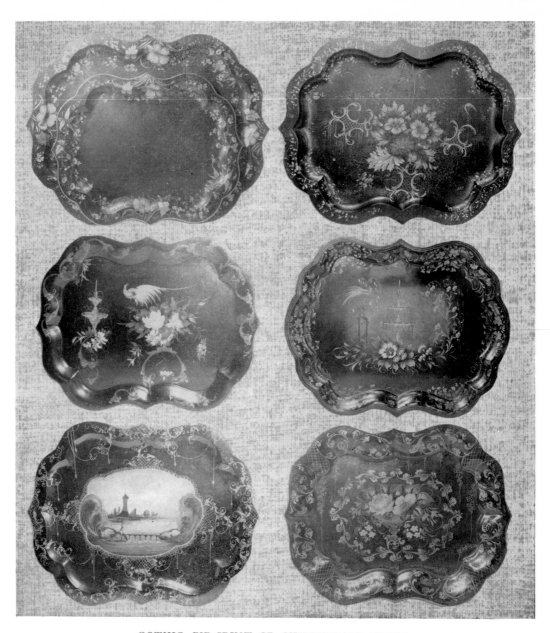

GOTHIC, PIE-CRUST OR CHIPPENDALE TRAYS

Upper left: Part of a nest of trays found under the eaves at 70 Beacon Street, Boston. Courtesy of Mr. Allan Forbes. *Upper right:* A "Sandwich edge" gothic tray. Courtesy of the Auburn Furniture Company. *Center left:* Gothic tray with scroll in dark red-brown and gold on black background. Courtesy of Mrs. Arthur Oldham. *Center right:* Gothic tray with separate gold-leaf sprays used as a border. Center design in color against gold bronze. Courtesy of Miss Helen Aspinwall Smith. *Lower left:* Another Sandwich gothic tray showing landscape tied in cleverly by gold scroll from the border. Date about 1825. Owned by Mrs. George Berkander. *Lower right:* Gothic tray with deep blue ground behind center pattern. Date about 1825. Owned by Mrs. Edward Cutler.

wire binding.) All types of painting from early delicate gold-leaf and bronze work to late stenciled bronze are found on these trays, as though they were popular through most of the periods in which we have an interest. The only kind of design that would look inappropriate on this form of tray is a lace-edge pattern.

CHIPPENDALE, PIE-CRUST OR GOTHIC TRAY

Mystery also surrounds the dating of a "pie-crust" or Chippendale tray, in spite of the fact that it undoubtedly originated in the 1760 Chippendale period. According to Mr. George Dickinson, who wrote on English papier-mâché, such trays were called "Gothic," and the varying patterns in the scalloping decided whether it was a "Queen's Gothic" or a "King's Gothic." If the outer section of the pie-crust edge (he calls it "gadrooned" edge) was flattened to a perfectly horizontal line, the term Sandwich was added to the title — thus the tray in illustration opposite page 149 would be called a "Sandwich Gothic" among the old-time japanners in Wales. Once this shape had developed, it continued to be made for many years, reviving to great popularity in the 1840's and 1850's when there was a decided Chippendale revival. An early Gothic tray, of the 1760 period, would undoubtedly display decorative design work full of painstaking detail and subdued coloring — one that would not be "showy," like the 1840 period was in all forms of artistic expression.

All grades of workmanship appear upon "Gothic" trays, as we should call them if we adopt the old-timer's terminology. Fine examples show intricate gold work quite evidently applied with a pen, in pendent "moss" and dripping vine patterns. Some of the most beautiful, vibrantly colored flowers appear on these trays through elaborate build-ups of transparent colors. Fountains of green-white water splash perpetually in the midst of these floral beauties. Birds of gorgeous plumage were usually hovering near, with filmy tails and iridescent colored breasts, which owe their brilliance to an underlying layer of silver or gold leaf. But there were also in later days many trays painted carelessly with large brushes and coarse workmanship. These clumsy versions the tray collector would do well to avoid as they are by no means up to our present standards of beauty.

Some Gothic trays, particularly those with the "Sandwich" flattened edge, were ornamented with floral sprays at the edge only, while the center was left entirely clear of decorative pattern. In all probability these trays date around 1800, when simplicity was the keynote of all decoration. We also note a great restraint in the use of color, which would further substantiate the 1800 date.

OVAL OR WINDSOR TRAYS

Then came the oval trays of a distinctly Victorian type with boldly rounding edge and often poor design work. These were called "Windsor" by the old japanners. Some few examples were finished most elaborately with the very finest of japanner's skill, but unfortunately not many of these beautiful examples are to be met with today. There seem to be thousands of the more ordinary oval trays which were painted black and decorated with odd sprays in gold leaf at intervals along the edge. Hundreds of others exhibit large gold scrolls combined with meaningless *ᴍᴍᴍᴍ* and a small bunch of flowers in the center. Sometimes mother-of-pearl inlay accompanied the design, providing basic high lights for roses and morning glories, or providing nothing whatsoever but a slight distraction.

All the above-mentioned types of tin trays were manufactured in quantity in rival shops at Pontypool, Usk, Wolverhampton, Birmingham and Aldermanbury, where metal and coal for the working of it were both available. That there were other less famous manufactories we haven't a doubt. The wares produced in England and Wales were designed as furnishings for fine homes, a city rather than a country type. Whether there were any similar manufactories in American cities, we are not certain. We suspect that Boston or Dedham, Massachusetts, had such shops for the manufacture of fine japanned ware, though the custom of affixing a maker's label was never adopted, and proof thereby is lacking.

COUNTRY OCTAGONALS OR "COFFIN TRAYS"

But, in America, we had the rural tinsmith who turned out a distinctive product of his own. His trays were generally octagonal, because these could be made without knocking into shape over-elaborate forms. The edge was decidedly narrow, and sometimes, to conserve tin, the larger trays were made with a central seam. It has been said that these are the *oldest* form of tray, but until we see one with the earliest form of painting on it, we will continue to doubt the accuracy of this statement.

Country tinsmiths decorated their wares in white, yellow, vermilion, blue, and green upon various colored grounds. Most usual, of course, were the

black and asphaltum backgrounds, but there were some instances of vermilion, dull red, bright yellow, transparent blue, and even white backgrounds.
To the country tinsmith, gold and silver leaf were practically unknown, so
also were bronzes until the 1820 period of stenciling took the stage.

COUNTRY TINWARE

Besides the octagonal tray with narrow edge, our country tinsmith turned
out boxes, tin sconces, match receivers, tea caddies, sugar boxes, teapots,
coffeepots, and many other articles space does not allow us to enumerate.
All were decorated similarly in gay colors with simple brush-stroke patterns.
It is amazing to see how closely the patterns of Connecticut tinsmiths follow
those of their confreres in Pennsylvania, in New Hampshire and in Maine.
Probably these designs were acquired during apprenticeship days, since many
learned their trade in Connecticut where tinsmithing early became famous.

Last of all, our country tinsmiths seem to have learned about bronze
stenciling, and to have turned out many simple pieces decorated for the
most part with cut-in-one stencil patterns. From this point on, all gay color,
all semblance of a country folk-art disappeared, and tinware began to consist
largely of plain collanders, dishpans, cake boxes and similar articles for
kitchen use.

PAPIER-MACHE

It should be said here that alongside of painted tin trays and boxes, similar
products were made in papier-mâché and decorated by the same japanners.
Some of the same dies were used to make both tin and papier-mâché pieces in
the same factory. The designs may be almost identical, for a japanner
sometimes "set" a pattern on which he collected royalty. The japanner's art
was the same, whether he used it upon a tin, wood or paper base.

PAINTED PEWTER

There was also the painting of pewterware, which is quite rare and seems
to have been made mostly in Holland. So far, we have never seen a japanned
pewter tray, but decorated candlesticks, hot coffee urns, and small boxes in
pewter are occasionally to be found in European antique shops. The designs
on painted pewter are identical with those on painted tin or papier-mâché of
the same period, which seems to have been from 1760 to the early 1800's.

PART FOURTEEN

The Painting of Colonial Woodwork

The Painting of Colonial Woodwork

THE widespread belief that paint was not extensively used in Colonial homes prior to 1725 is probably correct. Pigments were both scarce and expensive, while the supply of linseed oil seems to have been quite limited. But by 1750 there is ample evidence that most well-built homes were painted inside and out, while finer mansion houses often displayed elaborate examples of the decorator's art.

Before we go into details concerning Georgian period homes, we might say here that other-than-oil paints were probably used, occasionally, in earlier homes than the 1725 period, and continued to be used in far-off rural districts. In this connection, we refer to water paints, to whitewashes, and to casein paints made with that ample by-product of the farm, skim milk. We have found it difficult to resurrect old-time recipes for these mixtures, but all of them are available in modern forms, even to the casein paint. It has often been suggested that the old barn red was made from Indian red or from iron oxide mixed with skim milk (and probably some lime) which, surprisingly enough, does harden and become quite impervious to weather. We are all of us familiar with the same dull red on feather-edge boarding in old kitchens, and on a large quantity of country-made cupboards.

DECORATED CEILINGS

That another kind of water solvent[1] paint was used seems probable when we observe the ceiling paints in houses built around 1690. Here we find a sort of sponge dotting at intervals in black on a whitewashed, open-timbered ceiling formed by the supports of the second-story flooring. Or occasionally this coloring is reversed so that white sponge mottling appears on black! Sometimes the "pattern" is a crude herring-bone or zig-zag.

[1]Casein paint is water solvent in its early stages, but becomes washable after 30 or 40 days.

But, for the most part, the paint on Colonial woodwork was made of lead and oil similar to that described in our chapter on painted chests. In the old days, colors were obtained by decorators in dry powdered form, and were mixed with white lead, zinc, raw linseed oil and turpentine to the desired consistency. Nowadays we find the purchase of colors ground in oil or in japan to be more easily obtainable and more practical, there being little difference in the final result.

ORIGINAL COLORS

A widespread belief that ivory-white paint was customary in Colonial homes is being rapidly superseded. Now we have come upon ample evidence that other colors, frequently quite dark colors, were used fully as often as white paint on paneling in the Georgian era. Medium-toned blue, green, yellow ochre and gray were quite customary, besides the Indian red previously mentioned. Williamsburg furnishes us with a vivid memory of these bright colors for which they have done careful research. In Southern homes two tones were often used, a light one for the panels, and a slightly darker tone for stiles and rails that frame them, or vice versa. Southerners also painted mouldings around the panels a contrasting or decorative color. At Mount Vernon there is evidence that one or more important rooms were accented with touches of gold leaf in the carving. So also in the great central hall at Lee's home known as Stratford, where the magnificent Ionic columns painted a delicate *café au lait* were once adorned with gold leaf in their flutings. How decorative they must have been with the great brass H and L hinges, always kept polished to a shining gold color, ornamenting the adjacent cupboard doors!

TWO-TONED FINISHES

Then there were the two-toned finishes of graining and marbleizing. Here again Williamsburg found corroborative evidence. We remember seeing Northern homes, some unpretentious houses, some grand mansions, where panels were painted to imitate marble, cedar, and mahogany. Maine and New Hampshire can both boast of simple pine meeting-houses with columns mottled to simulate marble or panels grained like crotch mahogany. In such ship-building towns as Kennebunkport, Maine, and Duxbury, Massachusetts, doors were grained expertly by ships painters to look like real mahogany.

OVER MANTEL A FOCAL POINT

The over-mantel panel was quite apt to be elaborately adorned to make a focal point for the room, unless of course an ancestral portrait already hung there. Other important panels were sometimes landscaped — but here we are digressing from our subject, which concerns early American *design* rather than the fine arts.

DECORATED FLOORS

As for floors, the extent of fancy painting may never be fully realized. It is our belief, judging from perfect examples in the tiniest of story-and-a-half homes, that the "best" room in most old houses may have had a decorated floor. The earliest of these were painted freehand in simple or elaborate designs depending upon the quality of the home or the ability of the decorator. Then there were stenciled floors, some consisting of running borders only, others boasting additional allover center patterns in squares, diamonds or hexagons. We should make every effort to record traces of these designs while they are still visible, for little evidence has been collected and the rapid deterioration of painted floors causes many to be obliterated beyond recall.

STENCIL METHODS

Rufus Porter, in his handbook,[1] gives us an outline of procedure in the stenciling of floors that differs not one bit from modern vibrative brush stenciling. We may proceed in this manner if we so desire, but the stencil may be fragile, and the floor will consume hours of back-breaking labor.

We have developed by experiment, a faster, safer process based upon the bronze stenciler's use of velvet. We have found that by cutting our stencil in a thinner paper than stencil board, such as charcoal drawing paper, and toughening it with successive coats of shellac and varnish, we may apply the pattern with a piece of heavy drapery velour that has a deep pile. We use japan tube colors, plus oil color if desired, blended with a palette knife. Our medium is carbona poured bit by bit (to save rapid evaporation) in a small tin cover. The velour, wrapped around our index finger, is dipped in the carbona, then in the paste paint, rubbed out on a piece of waste paper

[1]"Curious Arts," published in Concord, N. H., 1826. (Quoted in the Addenda.)

till excess fluid has evaporated, and then is passed over the stencil. Thanks to carbona, it will be found that the back of our stencil seldom requires cleaning.

Frankly, we admit that this process does not follow old-time directions given in 1825. We are not accustomed to adopting or advising radically new methods, but the results of this carbona stenciling save so much time and give such convincing effects that we dare to suggest it. The stencil work so applied seems to have the same "thin" texture we have seen on old floors. A speedy form of stenciling is quite a boon in this modern day and age when decorators cannot work for their "keep" and a few extra glasses of rum! Needless to say, stenciled floors are given several coats of brown "antiquing" varnish, and kept carefully varnished thereafter, when wear begins to show.

The usual color for painted floor backgrounds is yellow ochre. This had a tendency to turn brown with the years till it became almost a natural wood color. It made an excellent base for patterns in black and white, in dull blue, in old red or medium green. Once we saw a soft green background, with a pattern of vermilion tulips in wreath formation, accented by black and creamy white rosettes. Another time we saw a gray floor with patterns in dark green and white. But medium-toned brownish yellow was the over-whelmingly popular background color.

MARBLED FLOORS

Floors were also painted to look like gray marble, with black and white veins realistically or fantastically painted. It is quite an art to strike in these veins pleasingly by dipping a feather quill into the veining color and using it instead of a paint brush. In some cases this veining is applied to a clear coat of raw linseed, turpentine and japan dryer so that the veining marks spread a little in cloudy indefiniteness. Less successful attempts at marbleizing seem to have been done with a brush. On Nantucket Island, we find simple versions of marbling in little fishermen's cottages at 'Sconset. In Hingham we find an "entry" floor painted with "slabs" of marbling in graduated gray tones. But in the General Gage house recently moved from Danvers, Massachusetts, to Washington, D. C., there came to light the very finest of marble-veined floors, with a splendid Georgian scroll border painted in black and white. Three other floors in this same mansion house were also decorated quite elaborately. Such examples in a home of wealth convince us that the decorating of floors was never meant to be a cheap substitute for rugs.

SPATTER FLOORS

If we do not mention the spattering of floors, which has become well known on Cape Cod, it will seem strange to many people. It is a quaint, simple and easily reproduced floor finish, lending itself to many color schemes. The variety of floor background colors, with contrastingly colored paint dots, is endless. A little experimentation will make us adept in rubbing a stick along the edge of a broad brush in such a way as to scatter dots quite evenly. *But* — and this is a big but — we do not believe that spatter-work floors antedate the 1840's or 1850's, which fact makes them seem to us out of place in a house of Colonial or Federal period.

HUNTING FOR A PATTERN ON A FLOOR

If we are arriving at the point of repainting Colonial woodwork, and wish to do some investigating to make sure of the original finish, we would proceed just as we do when hunting for designs on painted furniture. We would try washing with various solvents, usually denatured alcohol, or chipping carefully with a steel scraper. If we come upon something original and very interesting, we should save a small area by the way of evidence, cover it with a durable piece of cardboard (thumbtacked down) and proceed to reproduce the pattern over all the woodwork. Then, at any time the evidence is questioned, we may exhibit it easily by lifting the small piece of cardboard.

PRIMING COAT NOT A FINISH COLOR

Caution should be given here, in scraping woodwork for evidence of original color, that it took *two* or more coats of paint to produce a finish.[1] Thus, we often find a dull gray *priming* coat, an old red, or a yellow ochre. These paints were cheap; but we must not necessarily imagine that the room was originally finished in these colors. We must examine very carefully indeed the subsequent coats of paint to decide the *real finish*. Sometimes the colors are well enough paired to make their story clear. Sometimes there was a one-coat renewal. It is all very confusing. But if we come upon a paint that shows a quantity of fly specks, we may be sure that *that* was once a finish coat!

[1]Exception — Feather-edged boarding in early type homes may have had only coat of old red finish.

We are convinced that there was far more color in early American homes than most of us have realized. Bit by bit the evidence is coming to light, and we are piecing together a gayer picture of Colonial interior decoration. There is, for instance, a house in Portsmouth, New Hampshire, where ivory-white paneling sets off delicate Chippendale carving, painted crimson with touches of shining gold leaf. Similarly the capital building by Bulfinch, at Augusta, Maine, was originally adorned with Corinthian columns painted white, but gilded in the flutes, and gilded at the tips of curving acanthus leaves which surrounded a crimson "drum." The dining-room at the Harrison Gray Otis house was discovered to have been painted a beautiful soft green and bisque color on the panels, with all raised "London putty work" in the lighter tone like classic Wedgwood. So also was the ballroom at Mount Vernon painted in pale green and bisque in Wedgwood manner. At Stratford an important bedroom had soft green and old rose painted paneling. In a mill town near Providence, R. I., stands a fine house where the floor was painted an "ashes of roses" color, and a stencil design in turquoise and black was superimposed in a sort of basket-weave pattern.

And so the story goes! Color was just as important in the lives of our great-grandmothers as it is in the present generation. Whenever it was possible, their homes were attractively decorated, even if they had to wait years until a traveling decorator came their way.

On the opposite page is shown a stenciled floor that was found underneath straw matting in an old house at Newton, Mass. The house, built in 1734, changed hands in 1780, at which time the stenciling was probably executed, inasmuch as three other decorated floors came to light in the course of restoration.

Courtesy of PROF. ARTHUR S. DEWING

THREE DECORATED FLOORS FROM MASSACHUSETTS

At top: Section showing border in original condition on floor at Medfield, Mass., with detail tracing of same. *Center:* Same floor showing section of center pattern with detail tracing. Courtesy of Mr. George Dabney. *Lower left:* Stenciled floor in black, white and vermilion on medium green. House at Lunenburg, Mass., since destroyed by fire. *Lower right:* Stenciled floor with two borders and all-over center pattern; yellow ochre ground. Samuel Lincoln House, Hingham, Mass.

PART FIFTEEN

Early American Wall Decoration

Early American Wall Decoration

NO OTHER branch of the decorator's art brought more good cheerful color to our ancestors' homes than that of the fresco painter. Many were the traveling artists who went from one remote town to another looking for a prosperous farmhouse where they might find comfortable lodging as repayment for their labors. The great craze for wallpapers which arrived in the mid-eighteenth century, and continued for decades unabated, was responsible for the stenciled and freehand painted walls these itinerant decorators have left behind them. Wallpaper was fragile, and could be bought only in cities. It required an expert hand to hang it, once it had been carted over dusty roads to the little town, or to the remote farm on the hillside. But here, at the farm-wife's door, a pleading voice often begged for the chance to make her walls look "right smart and pretty." So in isolated sections all over New England, in upstate New York, in Ohio, in fact in most sections where the pioneer settler struggled to establish his home, we find reminders of itinerant artists who painted walls, but who bequeathed little else to posterity.

TYPES OF DECORATION

Some of these walls were decorated freehand with special borders accenting cornice, door and window trim, dado or baseboard; while a plain wall surface was left between, or an allover pattern was supplied like regular wallpaper. Other walls were done by stencils[1] which the decorator had ready cut in his tool kit, and sometimes tried out in the attic for the housewife's selection. Still other walls were adorned with landscape painting after the manner of fine imported wallpapers in the 1800 to 1840 period.

Directions for such "landscape painting on walls of Rooms" are given in the minutest of detail in a little book called "Curious Arts" published in

[1] Cf. *Early American Stencils* by Miss Janet Waring.

1825. The author, Rufus Porter, ought to have known what he was talking about inasmuch as he himself was a fresco painter in the vicinity of Boston (before he founded the *Scientific American*). It is even rumored that as a young man he put himself through Harvard by his fresco painting. The complete description from his book is quoted in our Addenda, for the benefit of those who wish to do a water-color fresco in landscape style.

WATER-COLOR PAINTS

But our chief interest lies in the simpler wallpaper type patterns. It goes without saying that *most* of this wall painting was a water-color paint, fixed with a certain amount of glue so that it would not rub off quickly. Stencils were applied with the same sort of mixture using an almost dry stencil brush so that the paint would not run behind the cut stencil board. Free-hand patterns were boldly applied with flexible design brushes similar to our ¾-inch quill brushes.

WATER COLOR OR OIL?

In doing a freehand or stencil wall today we must decide whether we want to put in our labor on a water-color wall which will be subject to all kinds of mischances and damage by moisture or whether we prefer to work in flat-finish oil paints that are more durable. A few old-time decorated walls were really done in oil color, and have withstood the ravages of time remarkably. Can we take these rare examples as an excuse to work in flat-finish oil paint today, or must we be "purists" and work only in old-time water color? Each man must decide this for himself. Those who feel that oil paint lacks the "soft" dusty coloring of water-color paint will stick by this mixture, and take their chances with the elements. They may even experiment with natural fruit juices in an attempt to match certain soft tones in old-time wall painting. For there is a persistent rumor in rural sections that berry juices were used by old-time stencilers. We can hardly imagine that professional decorators would not be using *pigments* for their work! Though the country housewife who occasionally managed to stencil her own walls might have turned to natural dye colors.

STENCILED WALLS IN OIL PAINTS

For those who decide that a flat-finish oil paint will be most satisfactory for their purposes, we suggest the use of thinner stencils, and the carbona-velour stencil process described in our last chapter. It may not be an

Two capitals (crated) by Bulfinch, for State Capitol, Augusta, Me. Courtesy of "Cappy" Stewart, Portsmouth, N. H.

Room in house at Newburyport, Mass., where the carving was gilded and accented in crimson.

Excellent Examples of Wall Stenciling

Stenciled room at the Bull Run Tavern, Shirley,
Massachusetts.
Courtesy of MR. ARTHUR DE LANGIS

Two views of stenciled walls at Washington,
Connecticut.
Courtesy of MR. RUSSELL JONES

PAINTED PLASTER WALLS

Upper left and right: Two views of a decorated hallway at New Gloucester, Me. Probably the work of Philip Rose, nephew of Paul Revere. Courtesy of Mrs. Robert F. Chandler.

Lower left: Stenciled borders in the Ichabod Goodwin House at Berwick, Me.

PAINTED WOODWORK

Upper left: House at Seaconnet, R. I., built in 1758. The decorated beam seems to hark back to a 1700-1725 period of crude early work. The marbling of panels on fireplace wall is still a bit primitive. Courtesy of Mr. Coombs.

Upper right and lower left: Two other views from same room showing doors painted at a later date, one with view of sea battle off Newport during Revolutionary War.

Lower right: Example of white sponge painting on black—an early ceiling finish found at Hingham, Mass. Cushing House, built about 1685.

authentic old-time method but it will work wonders in speed and accuracy, and produce the same general effect. Just what trick the old-time wall stencilers did use, we are unable to guess, but there is another rumor that they hung white sheets at the window to keep curious eyes from discovering their secret processes while they worked. In that case we might be excused for inventing a secret method or two ourselves.

PLOTTING THE DESIGN

Unless there is an old wall decoration to go by, we find it necessary to do much measuring and planning when we undertake a wall today. A piece of chalk and a yardstick are indispensable. First, the frieze stencil has to be decided upon, and centered on the chimney breast so that the ends of a unit are evenly "chopped off" if it does not measure out perfectly to the unit. Next we must run a stencil border around the window and door trim. A third border may run across the baseboard ending against the door trim border. Now the stripe pattern begins, if there is a stripe layout in the design we have selected. A long piece of string with dress weight or "plumb" attached, and a thumbtack at the other end, will be needed to guide our stripe in vertical position from frieze to baseboard or wainscot. The chalk and yardstick will be required to mark off well-spaced positions for the stripe to run. Last of all, we place the wheel rosette, or flower spray motifs that come with most of these stenciled stripe patterns.

SPECIAL TREATMENT OVER MANTEL

For over the mantelpiece, special elaboration was customary. Here we find extra large stencil units arranged in alternating positions, or a large bowl of stencil carnations spread forth in radiant color. Sometimes the stenciler transcended his art and dabbled in landscape fresco, with trees painted in delicate feathery sponge work. Yes, a small piece of sponge, especially selected because of its leafy suggestiveness, was dipped in foliage green to apply trees of peculiar exotic form. High lights were in yellow green and in chrome yellow. Then there were white houses with deep red roofs, and red fence posts in the front yard, and black-paned windows stenciled in carefully. Sometimes we find a whole village scene with many houses, country store and meeting house. And then sometimes we find a great ship painted in between dock warehouses as though the occupants of this home had had a keen interest in commerce.

If the design we wish to execute is freehand, we plan the entire skeleton of it with chalk lines for guidance. We *make* our frieze unit figure out to completion on each side of our wall, so that the corners look perfectly balanced. It is possible to stretch each unit an inch or two if necessary without its being noticeable, but an incompleted unit in a festoon border, for instance, is most disconcerting. Next we run our border around doors and windows, and complete panels if they enter into our calculations. It is customary to "stop" door and window borders *against* the frieze, unless there has been too little space above window trim to allow for the frieze. Where a very narrow space only is available above door and window trim, and the narrow border will just about fill it, then the wide frieze may be "stopped" against the narrow border which will run around three sides of these architectural frames.

DESIGN ABOVE DOOR AND WINDOW TRIM

When the space above the door or window is too wide for the narrow border, or too narrow for the wide frieze, Heaven help us! It will call all our ingenuity into play, or we will have to re-plan our entire decoration! Sometimes we must narrow our frieze to make things look reasonable. Once in a stenciled room we wiggled out of a tight problem by cutting a slightly smaller version which was made to fit on quite reasonably to the master unit. Needless to say, it is generally far simpler to find a solution if the wall is a freehand pattern.

PRACTICAL ART TODAY

Though it may sound strenuous, we would propose that this art of interior wall decoration be made a hobby for the modern woman. Not all wallpapers on the market today coincide with our needs as to pattern and color; they require the services of an expert paperhanger whenever we want them applied to our walls. But if we put ourselves to work in stenciling borders around mantel, door, and window trim, and a frieze around the cornice, we may achieve an interior that is satisfying from both the practical and the artistic viewpoints.

NEW EXAMPLES OFTEN COME TO LIGHT

In the present-day craze for rejuvenating old Colonial homes as country houses, more and more of these old-time patterned walls are coming to light.

When one is discovered under old wallpaper, we rush to record it before something happens to obscure it from view. If only we could persuade people to have a panel of wall board fitted neatly into place, secured by tiny turn buttons, before they repaper or paint the wall, then the design would be preserved from destruction. It is no trouble at all to paint or paper over that wall board panel when the rest of the room is done. Then all will look shipshape and tidily in order, yet the "evidence" will be preserved to the satisfaction of the most rabid antiquarian.

For pattern is the product of its period, and we will lose something of historical importance if we do not exert every effort to preserve these old-time decorations from oblivion.

PART SIXTEEN

*Practical Demonstrations of
Old-Time Technique*

Practical Demonstrations of Old-Time Technique

THE following section of this book is devoted to a step-by-step pictorial exposition of how we build old-time decorations. Much thought has been directed toward selecting as widely varied a group as possible, that the student may gain a comprehensive view of how paints were handled. By putting himself through the copying of all these designs as directed, the student will find that he has learned the fundamental principles of old-time decorating. It will be apparent that most patterns are achieved by a *combination* of the methods we have been describing singly in the foregoing chapters of this book. We hope to establish in new students an analytical habit of mind, that they may understand and dissect an original design into its component parts. As we have stated elsewhere, we have made it our mission to broadcast knowledge of these methods in the belief that many more original designs may be restored and thereby preserved for posterity.

In minor parts, there are occasional places where some other method of procedure than the one we describe might be found workable. However, deviating experiments should be reserved for the time when a student has become thoroughly experienced in the handling of paints, and has passed into the realm of master-craftsman. The chances are too great that the beginner will not realize how far his substitute method falls short of matching the original old-time decoration.

.   .   .   .   .

The technical difficulties of producing these color illustrations have given the engravers and printers an almost superhuman task. Each craft has its own highly specialized methods; between the painting of a design and the printing of it there is a wide gulf of mechanical differences. The author wishes to express here her appreciation of the labor involved in printing the ensuing color illustrations without which our study would be greatly handicapped.

To the patience, ingenuity and technical skill of Mr. John D. Pond and Mr. Carl N. Ekberg of The Pond-Ekberg Company, and to The Massasoit Engraving Company, under the direction of Messrs. Ector Rosati and Henry W. Plate, all of Springfield, Massachusetts, we owe this volume as it now stands.

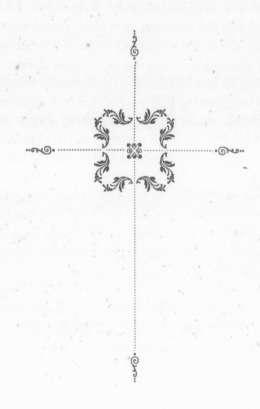

AN EXPOSITION OF OLD-TIME DECORATIONS

Courtesy of Mrs. Arthur Oldham

Example of a Single-Unit Stencil on a Four-Sided Apple Tray

PREPARATION

Paint the four-sided apple tray 2 coats of flat black paint, allowing each coat 24 hours to dry. Cut the two stencils as shown.

FIRST STAGE

Apply an even coat of 24-hour varnish if it is a fair weather day, or a coat of japan gold size if it is bad weather.

SECOND STAGE (about 1 hour later)

When varnish is almost dry, put these stencils in place and apply the desired aluminum bronze powder.

THIRD STAGE (24 hours later)

Take a large show-card brush and, with a small quantity of varnish, spread a tone of dull Prussian blue tempered with raw umber over the inner side of the right-hand flower. Take alizarin crimson and raw umber to similarly shade the outer side of the left-hand flower and the "peach" at top center of pattern. In each case, after applying the colored varnish, wipe the brush dry on a cloth and force the colored varnish to shade down to nothingness. Tone some of the smaller leaves green, using Prussian blue, yellow lake or gamboge and raw umber.

FOURTH STAGE (24 hours later)

Stripe around all four sides of the base and all four sides of each slanting panel. Use a mixture of chrome yellow light, yellow ochre and chrome yellow medium in varnish and the 1½″ striping brush. Striping may be applied sooner than indicated if the decorator can keep from laying hands or fingers in the newly-applied transparent color of Stage Three.

FIFTH STAGE — Not illustrated
(24 hours later)

Apply a coat of 24-hour varnish in which a little raw umber or raw umber and burnt umber have been mixed. Repeat varnish at 48-hour intervals until the desired antique tone is achieved.

SIXTH STAGE (48 hours after last varnish coat was applied)

Take pulverized pumice and crude oil with a soft cloth to rub down the shiny varnish surface. Remove all traces of oil and pumice with a clean, dry cloth which will leave a slight polish.

Example of Composite Stencil

USED IN OBTAINING THE DESIRED EFFECT IN THE TREATMENT
OF LEAVES AND BERRIES

Showing how veins of leaves and details on strawberries may be stenciled first, and the larger forms surrounding these details may be applied immediately afterwards. Be careful to let the top of each strawberry disappear into darkness. Use fire-colored bronze powder for the strawberry tips.

Stencil pattern demonstrated by Mr. George Lord, the old-time craftsman of Portland, Maine

The silhouette appears to have been one of the early forms of bronze stenciling and was generally enriched with freehand brush strokes in black or color

Reverse Stenciling or Silhouette

PREPARATION

Two coats of flat black paint as a background. Cut stencil as shown, trimming off outer edge to bird form last of all.

FIRST STAGE

Varnish the tray border; then take this stencil and lay in position when varnish is dry enough to stencil.

SECOND STAGE (1 hour later)

With stencil form in position, take piece of velvet and apply a completely surrounding cloud of silver powder. Lift stencil and add immediately internal clouds of fire-colored bronze powder to bird's body, wings and tail.

THIRD STAGE (24 hours later)

Take lamp black, mix with japan gold size, and apply with a fine ¾″ brush these fine stem lines and leaf sprays. Trim off the undesired sections of silver clouding with some of the original flat black paint with which the background was painted.

TYPE ONE   TYPE TWO

Practicing Stenciling of Leaves

Cut stencils as shown in each illustration, not omitting the two S curves on edges of pointed leaf stencil in Type One. Take practice paper well blackened with flat black paint.

TYPE ONE

FIRST STAGE

Apply a coat of 24-hour varnish and allow to dry until only slightly adhesive.

SECOND STAGE (1 to 2 hours later)

Place the leaf stencil in position and apply pale gold bronze with velvet-wrapped index finger. Stroke inward from outer points of leaf toward the center where it gradually fades into darkness. It is better to have more blackness at the center of this type leaf than ordinarily. Lift the stencil and place the S curve cut on the upper edge of our stencil (as illustrated below) in position as midrib of the leaf. Rub over the curving edge with shaded bronze powder to achieve the effect shown in center illustration. Next, move these S curves repeatedly, rubbing over the edge each time until the effect in the color illustration opposite is completed. This type leaf we sometimes call a modeled leaf. Needless to say, it requires more time and skill to execute than the Type Two leaf.

TYPE TWO

FIRST STAGE

Apply a coat of 24-hour varnish and allow to dry until only slightly adhesive.

SECOND STAGE (1 to 2 hours later)

Lay the leaf pattern in position and apply pale gold bronze with velvet-wrapped index finger. Stroke from the outer edge inward toward the center of leaf where the bronze disappears into nothingness. Remove the stencil, and place vein stencil in position at center of the leaf. Apply pale gold or silver bronze powder to the vein stencil. Let the veins disappear gradually when nearing base of leaf.

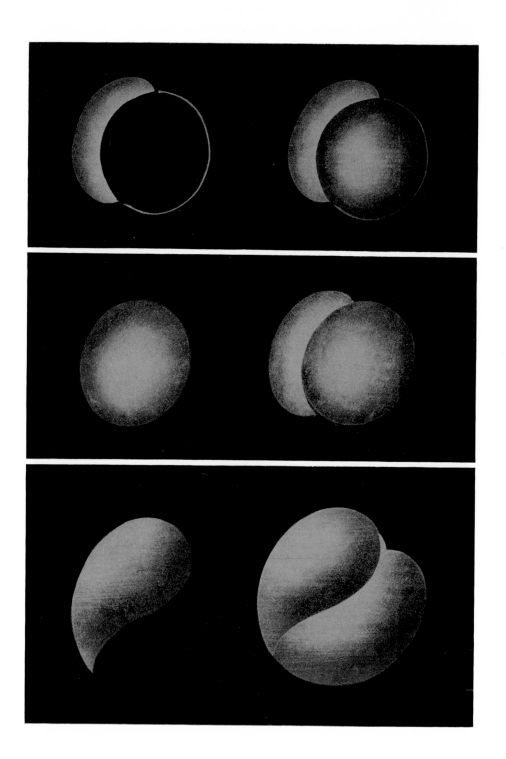

Three Types of Stencil Peaches

Varnish a piece of blackened paper and allow to dry from 1 to 2 hours until slightly adhesive.

TYPE ONE

The back section of peach and fine circular line are stenciled in first. Then the stencil is lifted and a circular high light is applied in center of circle. Care must be taken to make this high light well shaped and smoothly, gradually shaded.

TYPE TWO

The oval section of peach is stenciled first, accenting the center with plenty of bronze powder. Next the crescent form is added, brightly bronzed where it comes against the already stenciled section.

TYPE THREE

Upper left-hand section is stenciled in first, taking care to leave lower right in darkness. Next, the lower right stencil is put in position and bronzed with high light where it touches the central section already stenciled.

Examples of Stencil Flowers

Apply 2 coats of flat black paint to plain, unwrinkled paper, allowing 24 hours for each coat to dry.

TYPE ONE

FIRST STAGE
Apply a coat of 24-hour varnish to the blackened paper and allow from 1 to 2 hours for drying.

SECOND STAGE (1 to 2 hours later)
Lay the stencil in position and apply pale gold bronze powder, as shown on the left in illustration. Lift the stencil and cloud in an area behind the center of flower with fire-colored bronze powder.

TYPE TWO

FIRST STAGE
Same as foregoing first stage.

SECOND STAGE
Using stencil as shown, apply largest section first in pale gold bronze, shading from outer edges inward. Next add inner wreath in silver bronze. Lastly, apply the group of diamond-shaped dots in fire-colored bronze within the silver wreath.

Example of Multiple Stencil Rose

FIRST STAGE
Same as Stencil Flowers on previous page.

SECOND STAGE (1 to 2 hours later)
Using five stencil cuttings as shown, place the largest section first, and apply pale gold bronze powder around the outer edge, as in upper left example. Next, place the

"cup" form of the rose with its accompanying oval dot in position at center, and shade carefully with silver at the top edge, merging into pale gold at the base, as shown in lower left example. Add next the right inner petal, followed by the left, both in silver

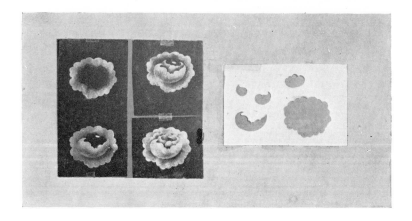

bronze, as shown in the upper right example. Lastly, add the scalloped petals which form the inner background, carefully shading each so that it may take its rightful position behind the previously stenciled "cup."

Courtesy of MRS. ARTHUR HOLMES

See the following pages for a detail description

Some Unusual Stunts in Stenciling

LEAF WITH SILHOUETTE STENCIL VEINS

FIRST STAGE Apply a coat of 24-hour varnish to a piece of black practice paper.

SECOND STAGE (1 to 2 hours later)

Place the leaf stencil in position, *with the silhouette veins turned back toward the center of the leaf,* before applying the bronze powder with velvet-wrapped finger. This will preserve the background color and keep the bronze powder from coming in contact. Next, lift the stencil and place the narrow line cut in position as a midrib to the leaf and apply bronze powder.

TRANSPARENT GREEN-BLUE SILHOUETTE LEAF

FIRST STAGE Apply a coat of varnish to a piece of black practice paper.

SECOND STAGE (1 to 2 hours later)

Using this silhouette leaf stencil, lay in position and cloud around the stencil with silver bronze powder. Lift the stencil and lightly cloud the interior of black leaf with pale gold bronze powder.

THIRD STAGE (24 hours later)

Apply a coat of dull transparent blue to the interior of the leaf. This pigment should be Prussian blue and raw umber mixed in varnish.

FOURTH STAGE (2 to 3 hours later)

When the green-blue varnish is *almost* dry, place this stencil in position directly over the other and apply pale gold bronze powder with velvet-wrapped finger.

TRANSPARENT BLUE FLOWER

FIRST STAGE

Apply a coat of 24-hour varnish to a piece of black practice paper.

SECOND STAGE (1 to 2 hours later)

First, stencil the whole form of this flower in silver bronze, as shown above.

THIRD STAGE (24 hours later)

Apply a coat of Prussian blue varnish over the previously stenciled form and allow to become *almost* dry.

FOURTH STAGE (2 to 3 hours later)

When the blue varnish is just slightly adhesive, lay the detail stencil in place and apply silver or pale gold bronze powder. The result is a beautifully clear metallic blue flower of high lustre.

TRANSPARENT ROSE-COLORED FLOWER

FIRST STAGE

Apply a coat of 24-hour varnish to a piece of black practice paper.

SECOND STAGE (1 to 2 hours later)

Take the silhouette form, second in the illustration below, and lay in position on the almost dry varnish. Apply a cloud of pale gold bronze powder around the form. Lift stencil form and apply faint clouds of pale gold bronze within the black silhouette, as indicated in third illustration.

THIRD STAGE (24 hours later)

Apply a coat of transparent rose-colored varnish over entire interior of poppy pattern, using alizarin crimson mixed with a little raw umber in varnish.

FOURTH STAGE (2 to 3 hours later)

When rose varnish is *almost* dry (just slightly adhesive), lay the detail stencil, shown at extreme left of illustration, in position over the silhouette and apply pale gold bronze powder with velvet-wrapped finger.

An Elaborate Grape Design Stenciled
on a Hitchcock Chair

PREPARATION Cut the group of stencils shown below.

FIRST STAGE
Apply a thin, even coat of varnish to a piece of black practice paper cut the same size and shape as chair slat.

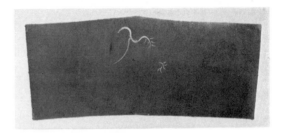

SECOND STAGE (1 to 2 hours later)
Begin composition by placing stem on which the grapes and large leaf are hung.

Progress by stenciling in the central grapes which show themselves as complete circles.

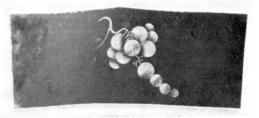

Add the flanking grapes one by one, working always from the center to those on the edge of the bunch.

Continue to add grapes in this fashion until the whole bunch is completed in natural form.

Next add the larger leaves, followed by the three little leaves as shown, remembering to leave center of leaf quite dark for the "modeling."

Tendrils may now be added — also the interior modeling of leaves, as shown in working illustration on the two following pages.

Adding the two side strips of conventional design completes the composition.

PLATE ONE

The painting of a typical Hitchcock chair begins with a coat of dull red paint over all the wood surface *except* the face of the main slat, which is given a solid coat of flat black paint.

PLATE TWO

Twenty-four hours or more after the red coat has been applied, graining begins. A coat of flat black thinned down with turpentine is applied. Graining is accomplished by pulling a crumpled piece of unbleached muslin across each

slat as it is painted. A second coat of flat black paint is given front of the main slat.

PLATE THREE

Twenty-four hours after the graining coat, stenciling may begin. A conventional design is generally applied to the upright stiles, turned top rail and front of seat frame.

PLATE FOUR

A mixture of gold bronze powder and varnish is used to accent larger turnings on the chair. Striping made from yellow and varnish is added last.

Example of Landscape Stencil on Fiddle-Back Chair

PREPARATION

Paint chair 2 coats of flat black, or 1 coat of dull red with overgraining of thin black. Cut the stencils illustrated here.

FIRST STAGE

Apply a thin, even coat of 24-hour varnish to the chair slat and allow to become almost dry.

SECOND STAGE (1 to 2 hours later)

Begin stenciling by laying the border which frames the landscape, using pale green bronze powder. Remember to clean the scroll pattern *on both sides* with paint remover before reversing the stencil.

Next, stencil the house and fence in pale gold bronze.

Add the overstencil to house in fire-colored bronze powder to represent brick. Proceed with the hills in the distance, trees and hillock in the foreground. The space between fence and hillock is filled lightly with bronze and does not require a stencil for the purpose.

Clouds of silver bronze are added in the sky. Small boats are stenciled in silver bronze. Two men, one leaning against a rock, are added to the foreground. A third tree is suggested between the two already placed in position.

No yellow stripe or broad band is necessary where the pattern is as completely framed as this.

(See color plate on next two pages)

Courtesy of MRS. JOHN OLDHAM

CHAIRS OF THIS
FIDDLE-BACK TYPE
DATE FROM 1840 TO
1860, AND MANY
WERE MADE IN
MAINE. MR. GEORGE
LORD DECORATED
SIMILAR CHAIRS
THROUGHOUT THE
LONG PERIOD OF HIS
ARTISTIC CAREER

Stencil and Freehand Paint Decoration on a Typical Yellow Chair Slat

PREPARATION

Paint chair 2 or 3 coats (3 is always preferable) of pale yellow, made from a mixture of flat white paint, yellow ochre, and a little Concord or chrome yellow in japan. Allow chair 24 hours to dry between each coat.

FIRST STAGE

Take a little lamp black in japan, mix with a small quantity of varnish and apply black form to fit the stencil pattern.

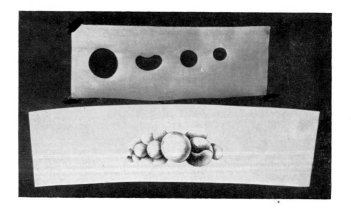

SECOND STAGE (1 to 3 hours later)

With stencil shown at the top, apply silver bronze as here indicated, commencing with the center fruit, then working outward to the extreme right and the extreme left.

THIRD STAGE (immediately)

Paint curving leaf forms, as shown here, in a dull olive green with a medium-sized show-card brush. Green is made from Prussian blue, raw umber, and chrome yellow, with japan gold size or varnish as a medium.

FOURTH STAGE (24 hours later)

Paint swirling tendrils in lamp black mixed with japan gold size — also the tiny detail lines on fruit and green leaves. Waiting for 24 hours permits the hand to be rested on the entire design without blurring the pattern.

FIFTH STAGE — Not illustrated (24 hours later)

Varnish the entire chair to protect the chalky finish from damage and provide a gloss surface for striping. It is possible to erase mistakes if a dry coat of varnish is on the chair. Also, stripes require a gloss finish on the background if we do not wish them to "creep."

SIXTH STAGE (24 hours later)

Apply a broad band of transparent brown (raw umber and burnt sienna usually) mixed in varnish. Follow this with a very fine black stripe 1/16 of an inch away from the band. Wait until the brown band has set thoroughly.

(See color plate on next two pages)

This pattern went through many variations. It was first found in gold leaf and freehand bronze on comb-back rockers from Portland, Maine; later,

Courtesy of MISS PURDY

used in this stencil version throughout
all parts of New England. The old
newspaper advertisements would have
called this a "Common Yellow Chair"

The original tray did not have this rose-colored jacket
which we have added to balance color.

A Large Stencil Landscape Tray

ILLUSTRATIONS HERE GIVEN ARE DONE ON BLACKENED PRACTICE PAPER

PREPARATION

Paint the tray 2 or 3 coats of flat black paint 24 hours or more apart. Cut the stencils here illustrated.

FIRST STAGE

Apply an even coat of 24-hour varnish and allow to dry in a level position.

SECOND STAGE
(1 to 2 hours later)

Measure long sides of the tray border and mark approximate center with a pencil or faint scratch mark. Place the silhouette stencil in this center position and, using velvet-wrapped finger, apply a cloud of pale gold bronze powder through and around the stencil. Next, place the floral border unit alongside and stencil as indicated in silver bronze.

Continue with border, each way from center of the long side up to the handle hole, then turn tray around, repeating stencil units until entire border is completed.

Begin center pattern by placing detail stencil of girl in swing and apply silver bronze powder.

On either side of the girl, place stencils of the two young men, with the hat which has fallen on the ground beneath the girl's feet.

Next, place the broad overtone stencils on top of these young people, moving each section till it fits into place perfectly. The faces are stenciled in silver bronze powder, the clothing and hat in pale gold.

Next, stencil in the branch, from which the swing is hung, in orange or copper bronze. Add the two flanking flower sprays in pale gold.

Apply the shaded tree trunk at the left in shaded orange or copper bronze. Add the grape arbor at the right in orange bronze, allowing it to disappear in shadow where it runs behind the flower spray.

Add the slender branch and leaves which cross the standing tree trunk, repeating the spray of leaves at top of trunk and just above head of young man at the left. Begin stenciling the field of flowers, as shown by single unit at lower left. All this stenciling is done in silver bronze.

Continue placing the field of flowers stencil until the whole groundwork is complete.

THIRD STAGE
(24 hours later)

Take Prussian blue, yellow lake, and burnt sienna in oil, with a show-card brushful of varnish, and color the border where indicated. Use burnt sienna to tint the children's hair and (with a fine brush) to make their individual facial details of eyes, nose, mouth and chin lines. Color the jacket on boy at left Prussian blue tinged with enough yellow to make a deep turquoise shade — on boy at the right, a soft rose color with alizarin crimson. Take a large brushful of deep blue green (transparent) in varnish and sweep through the field of flowers near the bottom. Into this, work immediately some burnt sienna and, lastly, yellow ochre and chrome yellow, so that the top of ground directly under the boys' feet is more solid and substantial in opaque pigment. Next, take a broad "foliage brush" and a semi-transparent green, made from Prussian blue, chrome yellow light, raw umber, and varnish, to pounce in the green foliage as indicated, high-lighting with the usual addition of chrome yellow.

FOURTH STAGE (24 hours later)

Place a broad band on floor of the tray, about ⅜″ from the bend where edge begins. Mix this paint with varnish and brown gold bronze, or green bronze powder, and apply with fine striping brush in two parallel lines, filling in with larger show-card brush. Add a fine yellow stripe just within the bronze band and at either edge of the border. Make this yellow of varnish mixed with chrome yellow light and yellow ochre to the desired shade. When these stripes have set, take flat black paint and trim off all undesired marks and unnecessary bronze powder, particularly around the silhouettes in the border.

FIFTH STAGE (24 hours later)

Begin varnishing the tray with 24-hour varnish toned with burnt umber and raw umber. Continue this process, allowing 48 hours between successive coats, until the desired mellow tone has been achieved. Then sandpaper carefully to remove blemishes and specks (using #00 sandpaper) and apply a coat of Super Valspar to alcohol-proof the work. Lastly, rub down with pulverized pumice and crude oil, polishing off all pumice with a clean, soft cloth.

Freehand Bronze and Stencil Pattern for a Bellows on a Smoked Background.

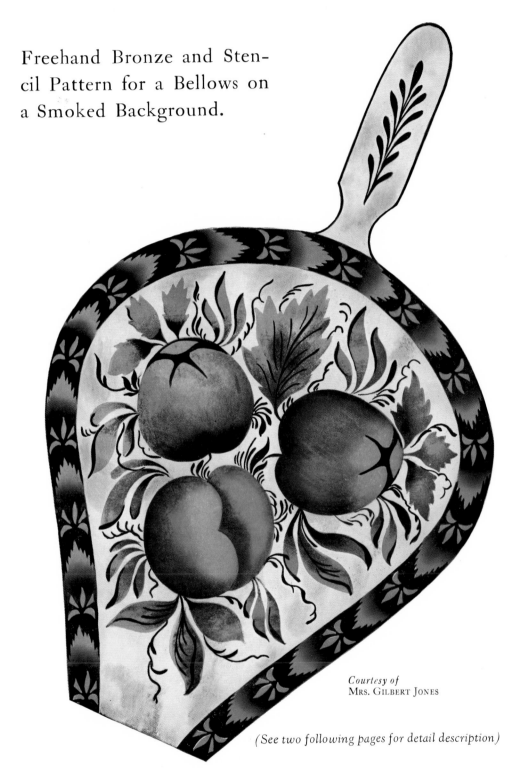

(See two following pages for detail description)

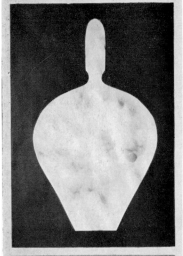

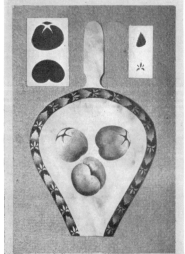

Freehand Bronze and Stencil Pattern on Smoked Background

PREPARATION

Two or 3 coats of flat white paint, toned with yellow ochre.

FIRST STAGE

Smoke the background by holding a candle against the bellows momentarily. More of the smoking will be retained if the bellows are given a coat of japan gold size or varnish, into which the smoke is forced just before drying.

SECOND STAGE (24 hours later)

Take lamp black in japan and a little varnish to paint the three main fruits and border with a fair-sized show-card brush.

THIRD STAGE (about 1 hour later)

When sticky black is *almost* dry, take these stencils and brush in a small quantity of pale gold bronze, merging with orange gold bronze as dark shadows are approached. Use a piece of stenciling velvet when applying this shaded bronze powder.

FOURTH STAGE (24 hours later)

Paint in larger leaf patterns with a similar mixture of lamp black and varnish, as here indicated, using a small ¾″ quill brush.

FIFTH STAGE (about 1 hour later)

Take a piece of velvet and tip these large black leaves with pale gold bronze without using any stencil.

SIXTH STAGE (24 hours later)

Paint in the last fine black strokes with a tiny ¾″ quill brush and the same mixture of lamp black and varnish.

Small black stripe and leaf spray on the handle may be done either at the fourth or sixth stage.

FINISH

Finish with brown-toned varnish as in previous examples.

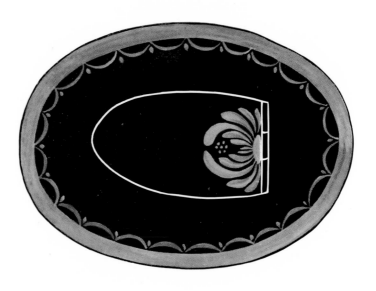

Courtesy of Miss Adeline Joyce

Simple Brush-Stroke Decoration
on a White Band

PREPARATION

Teapot painted two coats of flat black paint—24 hours allowed for each coat to dry.

FIRST STAGE

Apply an even white band made from Phillips white (in oil) and varnish. Apply with a large show-card brush, evenly, with long, straight strokes.

SECOND STAGE (24 hours later)

With a fine ¾″ quill brush, paint alternate groups of vermilion and green leaf strokes on the white band, as shown in color plate opposite. Vermilion is toned down with a little raw umber. Green is made from Prussian blue, raw umber and chrome yellow, mixed with japan gold size. Single dots at top of the band are in green. Next, take a fine 1½″ striping brush to run a vermilion stripe just above the bottom of white band. Below the white band, run two narrow yellow stripes, filling in between with a ¾″ quill brush dipped in the same yellow paint. This yellow is a mixture of chrome yellow light, chrome yellow medium, yellow ochre, and varnish. Then, with a small ¾″ quill brush add the tiny festoon stroke and dot which finishes the border. Apply the same border around base of teapot. Next, paint in yellow the group of strokes at cover hinge. Last of all, apply the band and festoon border around top edge of teapot.

Stencil and Freehand Bronze Pattern on a Medium Green Background

PREPARATION

Paint the background 2 coats of green made from coach painters' green and chrome yellow in japan, raw umber and white, mixed with turpentine and a little varnish.

FIRST STAGE — Not illustrated

Take lamp black in japan and varnish to paint entire silhouette of leaves and grape pattern.

SECOND STAGE (about 1 hour later)

Take these stencils and apply pale gold bronze powder, commencing with the turned-up tips of each leaf, then progressing to the back form of the large center leaf. The grapes are then applied one by one. Last of all, the free standing leaves are tipped with bronze powder.

This box pattern illustrates how black was painted behind bronze stenciling when this method of decoration was to be used on colored backgrounds. In this example, the shape of each flanking leaf was carefully painted in the form it was to have when high-lighted at the tips with bronze powder.

Stencil and Freehand Bronze Pattern — *Continued*

THIRD STAGE (24 hours later)

Take chrome yellow and Concord yellow in japan, mixed with japan gold size, and paint in fine veins in the leaves, dots on the grapes, and scrolling tendrils.

Next, paint border ½-inch wide around all outside edges, both of cover and body of the box. Border is made of vermilion in japan, toned down with a little raw umber mixed with varnish. When this vermilion border is almost completely dry, take the tiny stencil illustrated above and add bronze powder by constantly repeating the stencil leaf until the entire circuit is completed.

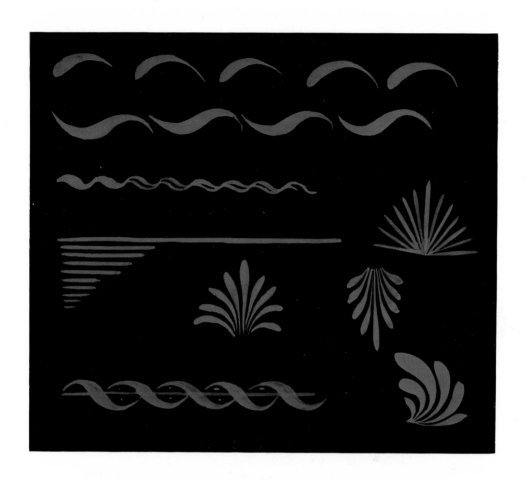

BRUSH-STROKE PAINTING

These exercises with small brushes will go a long
way toward teaching command of paint, brush and
sizing. All of these units are done with the small
¾″ square tipped quill brush, mounted on a handle.
Pigments are mixed only with japan gold size or
varnish — no turpentine is used whatsoever.

From the Author's Stevens Plains Collection

Example of Small Tea Caddy with Brush-Stroke Painting

PREPARATION
Tea caddy painted 2 coats of flat black, each coat allowed 24 hours to dry.

FIRST STAGE
Take chrome yellow in japan and yellow ochre in oil; mix with japan gold size. Using a medium-sized ¾″ hair brush, paint the three flowers and the brush-stroke border around the top of caddy.

SECOND STAGE (24 hours later)
Take vermilion and a little dark red in japan tube color; mix with a little raw umber in oil and some japan gold size. With a very fine ¾″ brush, paint the fine stem lines as shown in color plate opposite.

Next, take a larger ¾″ brush and paint the bolder, fatter leaf strokes. Lastly, return to the finer brush for painting the "tendril" off the tip of large left-hand leaf and the fine strokes around the flowers.

Courtesy of Mrs. Nina Fletcher Little

Example of Tin Candle Sconce

BRUSH-STROKE PAINTING

PREPARATION

Two coats of flat black paint, each allowed to dry for 24 hours.

FIRST STAGE

Take vermilion in japan color, mix with japan gold size, and apply the six "flowers" with a medium-sized, ¾″ hair brush.

SECOND STAGE (24 hours later)

Take chrome yellow in japan, Prussian blue and raw umber in oil and mix a dull green with japan gold size. Use a small ¾″ hair brush to apply the curving stem and leaf strokes that appear in the dark color. Take Phillips white, yellow ochre and raw umber in oil, mix with sufficient gold size to make the pigment quite transparent, and apply the light-colored leaf strokes. Likewise apply high lights with the same dull white upon the flower forms. Lastly add the vine-like borders in dull white.

THIRD STAGE (24 hours later)

Take alizarin crimson and raw umber in oil, mix with japan gold size and apply transparent overtone upon the blossoms, working in dull white accents as desired. Add the dull whitish green touches to leaves and stem line.

FINISH

As usual, finish with several coats of brown varnish and rub down with pumice and crude oil.

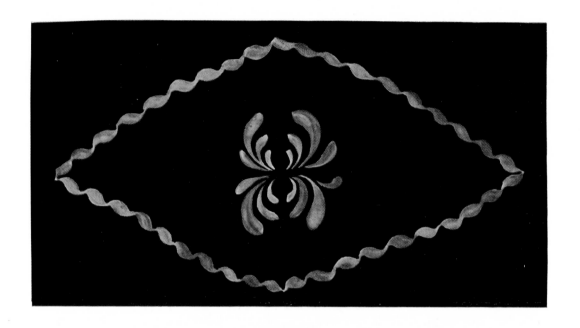

Courtesy of MRS. ELIZABETH ANGIER

Example of Country Tin Box

SIMPLE BRUSH-STROKE DESIGN

PREPARATION

Two coats of flat black paint, each allowed 24 hours to dry.

FIRST STAGE

Take vermilion in japan, mix with varnish, and apply these flower and bud forms quickly and smoothly with a fair-sized show-card brush. Too small a brush will leave the flowers streaky. Mixing with gold size would also leave the flowers streaky, as these are large areas to spread evenly.

SECOND STAGE (24 hours later)

Take alizarin crimson and raw umber in oil, mix with varnish and, with a show-card brush, apply the dark shading on the tulip. With a medium-sized ¾" hair brush, apply the dark shading on rose and buds. Next take chrome yellow in japan, Prussian blue and raw umber in oil, mix with japan gold size (or varnish) and apply the green leaves and fine stem lines. It is always well to apply stems first, so that the leaves may "grow" off of them naturally.

THIRD STAGE (24 hours later)

Take Phillips white, mix with varnish until quite transparent, and apply the high lights on the tulip, as in the color plate opposite, taking care in shading away that brush strokes follow natural curves of the flower. Next apply high lights on rose and rosebuds. Then take ivory black in japan color, mix with japan gold size for fast setting, and apply the fine black veins in the leaves. For the yellow borders, mix chrome yellow in japan and yellow ochre in oil, with japan gold size in a small cup so the mixture is smooth and of the right density. Take a small ¾" brush and draw a line down center of the box lid upon which to build the leaf stroke and dot border. Lastly, place the leaf stroke pattern in center of the cover around the wire handle and frame it with the diamond pattern reverse-S stroke. If the black veins in the leaves are well set by now, add the fine yellow veins and the tiny high lights on smaller leaves.

Finish as usual.

From the
Author's Collection

Tea Caddy (with Transparent Rose Background)

PREPARATION

If tea caddy is in bright tin, no preparation is required. If tea caddy is dull, apply a coat of varnish and, when almost dry, apply silver-colored bronze powder with a piece of velvet. This simulates bright tin.

FIRST STAGE (24 hours later)

Take ivory black in oil, thin with varnish or japan gold size and apply "graining" with a medium-sized show-card brush.

SECOND STAGE (24 hours later)

Apply a coat of varnish tinted with alizarin crimson and a little of gamboge and raw umber.

THIRD STAGE (24 hours later)

Take Phillips white and varnish to apply the large flower and tiny white flowers and buds. Add the green leaves made of chrome yellow in japan, raw umber and Prussian blue in oil, and japan gold size (or varnish). Apply the white striping.

FOURTH STAGE (24 hours later)

Take Prussian blue, raw umber and Phillips white, all in oil, mix with japan gold size and apply fine-line details to large flower. Add dots of blue to the other flowers and buds.

FIFTH STAGE (24 hours later)

Take chrome yellow in japan, mix with japan gold size and apply fine yellow lines with a tiny brush. Dot the center of the flower. Then pick up a striping brush and apply a broad yellow band at both edges of the cover and at bottom edge of tea caddy.

SIXTH STAGE (24 hours later)

With alizarin crimson and varnish apply the diagonal, transparent shading over the yellow band (see color plate), wiping out the brush dry when disappearance of the rose color is required.

Finish as usual.

Simple Border on Gold-Leaf Band

A PEN OR SNUFFER TRAY

PREPARATION

Paint the snuffer tray with 2 coats of flat black, 24 hours apart.

FIRST STAGE

Take japan gold size and pale gold powder and mix in a small cup. Apply two gold-bronze stripes of this mixture with a striping brush and fill in solidly between stripes, spreading mixture evenly.

(If protection for gold leaf is desired by the novice, then apply a coat of varnish 24 hours later. This will permit erasures to be made with carbona.)

SECOND STAGE (24 hours later)

Take alizarin crimson and varnish to apply the transparent rose form at left end of tray. Likewise apply Prussian blue and varnish at right end for the morning glory blossom.

(See next two pages for color plate and further description)

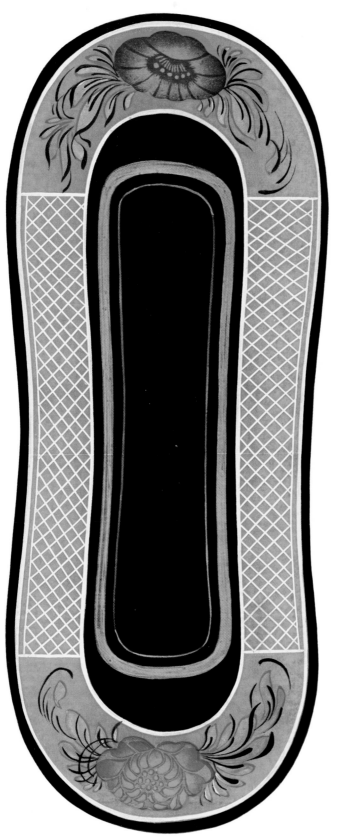

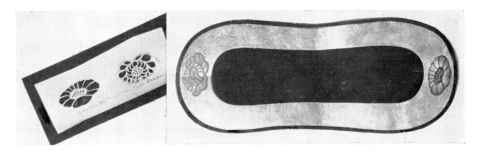

THIRD STAGE (about 3 hours later)

Test the crimson and blue lightly with the finger and, if it is almost dry, apply the two stencil units — pale gold bronze on the rose; silver bronze on the morning glory.

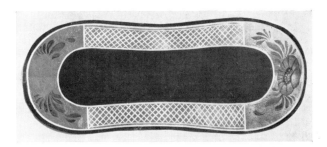

Take verdigris, raw umber and japan gold size with a small ¾″ quill brush and add the transparent green leaves at each end of the flowers.

Take Phillips white mixed with varnish to apply the fine white striping and lattice work. It will be easier to stripe if the transparent colors are fully dry so that the hand may be rested against the tray more completely.

FOURTH STAGE (24 hours later)

Take ivory black in japan and some japan gold size, with a fine ¾″ brush, and apply the fine black lines as indicated. Then mix a yellow ochre band and stripe color with varnish to complete the decoration. (See color illustration.)

Finish as usual.

Design for a Bordered Tray, such as may be found on heavy-bordered octagonal or early rectangular curved-corner trays

·{ 234 }·

Gold-Leaf Bordered Tray

PREPARATION

Paint the tray 2 or 3 coats of flat black paint, 24 hours or more apart.

FIRST STAGE

Take a small cap; make a smooth mixture of fast japan gold size and 24-hour varnish, half and half, adding a small quantity of bronze powder or japan paint (any color desired) for visibility. Paint the following design, commencing with the larger units, such as the flowers, shell and thistle leaves. Use a fairly thick ¾″ quill brush which is still fine enough to achieve the well-defined points on thistle and thistle leaves. Do not allow the sizing to "pool" anywhere, but spread thinly and evenly. Then take a very fine ¾″ quill brush and apply the tiny leaves and stem lines last, as these will dry more rapidly than the larger areas.

SECOND STAGE (as soon as fairly dry — about ½ hour)

Take a sheet of gold leaf on transfer tissue and lay upon the pattern, pushing gently with a piece of stencil velvet behind the tissue. Lift the gold-leaf tissue (which will now be minus the metal already adhered to the pattern), and move along to a new position where remaining gold leaf may be made use of. With a light touch of the velvet (so as not to mark or mar the smooth gilded design), make undesired sections of laid gold leaf come free of the pattern. This illustration below shows, at the right, pattern as laid in sizing; center, gold leaf freely adhering to the pattern; and left, the pattern in smooth gold leaf after excess metal has been lifted away with the velvet.

THIRD STAGE (24 hours later)

Take a drawing pen, or sharp-pointed metal tool, and etch the detail lines here and as shown in color plate. Then take a little burnt sienna and burnt umber or raw umber, mix with a little varnish, and add the brown shading as indicated. Border with a narrow yellow stripe.

Japanner's Design on Small Bellows

Paint background a medium blue-green made from coach painters' green in japan, toned with a little raw umber, chrome yellow and a little vermilion to neutralize the tone. If coach green is a very dark shade, a little flat white paint will be desired. Allow 24 hours for background to dry.

FIRST STAGE

Take gold size and a little pale gold bronze powder, applying with a small brush according to the design here shown. Striping brush should be used for the edging band. When proper stage of dryness has arrived, lay the gold leaf.

SECOND STAGE (May follow immediately if hand is kept from scarring the gold leaf)

Take flat black paint "paste" (from bottom of the can) and mix with Super Valspar in a small cup. Be sure mixture is completely stirred to achieve an even combination. Paint in black areas as here shown and let stand till almost dry.

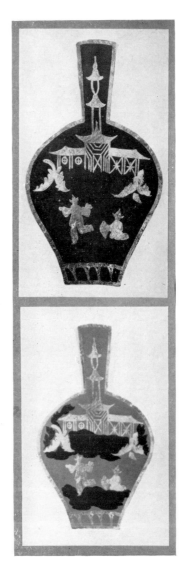

THIRD STAGE (When black is slightly tacky)

Take stencil and place as indicated, applying silver bronze with velvet-wrapped finger.

FOURTH STAGE (Immediately after above)

Apply orange-to-brown colored bronze powder at other edges of the black as indicated. Then take a very fine brush to apply lines in black on the figures, pagoda, etc.

FIFTH STAGE (24 hours later)

Take gum arabic mixture and apply fine gold lines of pine trees, kite string and tail, etc., with a crow quill pen. Allow gum arabic to set, according to instructions on pages 35 and 83f, and apply pale gold bronze powder by means that are directed by humidity present in the atmosphere. Then take burnt sienna, burnt umber and japan gold size to make transparent brown shading on the gold leaf pattern.

FINISH (After 24 hours)

Apply several coats of slightly brown-toned Super Valspar, allowing from 24 to 48 hours between each, and rub down with pumice and crude oil.

Lace-Edge Tray Pattern

Courtesy of Mrs. Edward R. Cutler

(Piercing of lace edge not drawn)

(See two following pages for detail description)

Lace-Edge Tray Pattern

PREPARATION

One or two coats of flat black paint applied 24 hours apart.

FIRST STAGE

Place irregular patches of japan gold size on the flat black background. When so dry as to be but slightly adhesive, lay sheets of silver leaf and brush away unadhered metal with piece of stencil velvet. (See illustration at left below.)

SECOND STAGE — Not illustrated   (24 hours later)

Cover the entire floor of the tray with a coat of Super Valspar made violently red with alizarin crimson in oil.

THIRD STAGE   (24 hours later)

Cover the entire tray with a coat of asphaltum varnish just as it comes from the can and, with a crumpled cloth (not too soft), lift out some of the asphaltum in irregular mottled patches. This makes what was called a "tortoise shell" background. (See illustration at right, below.)

FOURTH STAGE   (24 hours later)

Take English vermilion in japan and Super Valspar for the three flower spots. Use a show-card brush so that the larger spot may be evenly spread. Take Prussian blue, raw umber and yellow lake and a tiny touch of Phillips white to make dark green leaves grouped at center. Next, take Prussian blue, raw umber and white to make the single dot and stroke part of border shown at left on opposite page.

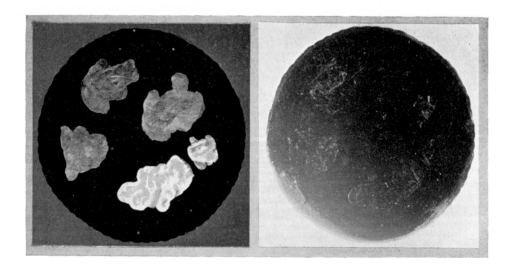

FIFTH STAGE (24 hours later)

Take 24-hour varnish and cover quite liberally with the show-card brush, one blossom only. Immediately work in alizarin crimson on the shadow side of blossom, Phillips white toned with yellow ochre and raw umber on the high-light side of blossom. Wipe out brush on a cloth and make these colors combine with an easy transition. Take vermilion, Phillips white, raw umber and a little yellow ochre to make the soft peach color for stems, tendril and the pair of dots in the border. Stripe is also made of this peach color.

SIXTH STAGE (24 hours later)

Take japan gold size and mix a dark semi-transparent green (to match the leaves) from Prussian blue, raw umber, yellow lake and Phillips white. With the small "hair pencil" brush apply calyx part of blossoms and the curving leaf spray, also the two green stems. Then pick up a little white and yellow lake with the green to make a lighter tone and apply the lighter overtones on the center green leaves and the rosebuds. Take Phillips white, raw umber and yellow ochre to make the dull white strokes in the border and the high lights on the rosebud calyxes.

FINISH (24 hours later)

Two or more coats of Super Valspar varnish toned with the transparent colors of alizarin crimson, yellow lake and Prussian blue to a light golden brown age color.

Rub off final gloss with pumice and crude oil.

A Gothic or Chippendale Tray

WITH FLOWERS IN COLOR ON A GOLD BRONZE BACKGROUND

PREPARATION   Two coats of flat black paint applied 24 hours apart.

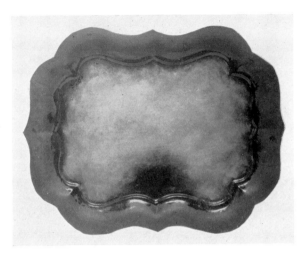

FIRST STAGE

Varnish "floor" of tray and allow it to stand until *almost* dry. Then rub on bronze powders beginning with a pale gold cloud at the center. Next, go to outside edge where disappearance of darkest shade of bronze powder is to be achieved. Fill in toward the center cloud with graduated shades of bronzes, through orange-gold to the pale gold.

SECOND STAGE (24 hours later)

Take japan gold size and pale gold bronze powder and, with a fine brush, apply the gold scroll and fountain here shown. Bon Ami powder protection around area of fountain is desirable. Apply gold leaf when ready.

THIRD STAGE (Immediately)

Next, take japan gold size mixture and paint in the form of bird and tail. Allow proper stage of dryness to be achieved and then lay silver leaf. Next, take Phillips white and varnish to lay in first stage of flowers, including the tiny buds that are scattered through the scroll work. With chrome yellow, raw umber and Prussian blue,

mixed with varnish, paint in the yellow-green leaves. Pick up more Prussian blue and raw umber to make a darker color and paint in the dark green leaves. Stripe exterior edge of tray with green-gold bronze powder and varnish.

FOURTH STAGE (24 hours later)

Lay out the transparent colors of alizarin crimson, yellow lake, Prussian blue, verdigris and burnt umber. Pour varnish out into a small cup and select a square-tipped

show-card brush for applying the colors. Beginning with the morning glory, apply a generous coat of varnish over the entire flower. Then work in the transparent yellow lake at the center, graduating it through orange to flame color, and tone the edges of the flower with Prussian blue. Similarly apply the blue and yellow only on the morning glory buds. On the large single dahlia, place the light tones of crimson and deepen boldly with burnt umber. Remember that the colors are put into the varnish in an almost dry form and a wiped-out brush is used to blend two different colors with subtlety. Place rose-colored tip on flower buds at the right. Similarly tone the rose and blue buds that are scattered through the gold scroll work. Place a generous coat of varnish over the bird and work in the tones of crimson, yellow-green and blue that are shown. Ends of the tail and wings have a little Phillips white worked in to the blue to make it a bit opaque. A tone of green-white is placed on the top of fountain to represent water. With a smaller brush-stroke brush put on a burnt sienna tone at right side of fountain and its pedestal. Burnt umber and black, mixed with varnish, should be used to shadow both the yellow-green and blue-green leaves.

FIFTH STAGE (24 hours later)

With Phillips white and a fine brush apply fine detail lines on the bird. Add the black eye and beak. Take chrome yellow and sizing for the bright yellow center in the dahlia. Also apply small chrome yellow dots in the buds that are scattered through the scroll. Take Prussian blue and alizarin crimson for sharp accent lines shown on the morning glory and its buds. Take Phillips white, raw umber and yellow ochre to apply lighter accents on the leaves. Add a bit more white to this mixture and make the dripping water of the fountain.

SIXTH STAGE (24 hours later)

With alizarin crimson place rounding shadow on the chrome yellow center of the dahlia, using show-card brush and varnish. Next, take chrome yellow and a very fine brush-stroke brush to apply fine yellow lines that curve outwards from this center.

FINISH (24 hours later)

Apply as many coats of varnish toned *slightly* with burnt umber, raw umber and black as seem desirable, allowing 24 to 48 hours between each coat. Rub down final coat with pumice and crude oil.

From a natural color photo, by the Author,
of a signed Christian Seltzer Chest formerly
owned by the Author

Pennsylvania Dower Chest

PREPARATION

Clean off all old paint from the chest and wipe down with turpentine.

FIRST STAGE

Paint the two panels with flat white paint. Repeat with a second coat at least 24 hours later.

SECOND STAGE (24 hours later)

Make a mixture of raw linseed oil and a few drops of japan gold size in a small cup to use in applying the following design colors. Mix ivory black and Phillips white for the two dark gray vases. Burnt sienna and burnt umber combine to make the stems and leaves of flowers. Use clear yellow ochre for yellow on parts of the flowers. Mix vermilion and raw umber for dull orange-red on flowers. Combine Prussian blue and raw umber for blue on flowers. Make a soft, transparent red of alizarin crimson and raw umber for the outline part of scroll border around the panels. Mix with raw linseed oil, turpentine and a little japan gold size a dull red from vermilion, raw umber and alizarin crimson for background of the chest and paint this on, swinging carefully around the panels and escutcheon, if the latter is not removed. When the dark gray vases are dry enough to retain the mark, take the blunt wooden end of a small brush handle and mark name, date, or pattern on the vases. Paint the bracket feet and bottom of moulding black.

THIRD STAGE (4 to 7 days later, at least)

Using the same color combinations as described just above, complete the flower petals, etc., that were not put in before, as they touched already executed sections and might have "run" together. Take Prussian blue and raw umber for the central part of the bordering scroll. Paint the thumb-nail moulding around the lid with this blue, made opaque with some Phillips white. Also paint upper part of base moulding blue.

FOURTH STAGE (14 days later)

Paint second coat of dull red background on the chest, swinging around the panels as before. Give the feet a second coat of black mixed with raw linseed oil and a little japan gold size. Wait a few days and then give the blue mouldings a second coat of dull blue.

FIFTH STAGE (14 days later)

Begin "antiquing" the chest by rubbing it with a soft cloth dipped in raw linseed oil and raw umber. Repeat these age coats every two or three weeks until the chest takes on a satisfactory semblance of age.

FINIS

ADDENDA

THE CABINETMAKER'S DICTIONARY

*[Notes from a Treatise on Painting by Thomas Sheraton,
published in 1803]*

Of Painting Furniture

The principal thing which constitutes this a distinct branch of painting is the general use of size and varnish colours, by which it is performed with much greater dispatch and effect. Yet the prices allowed in this country, at least in many parts of it, are so poor that the painter can hardly distinguish furniture from common oil painting.

Of Painting Chair Seats

Rush bottom chairs ought always to have their seats primed with common white lead, ground up in linseed oil and diluted with spirits of turpentine. This first priming preserves the rushes, and hardens them; and to make it come cheaper, a second coat of priming may have half Spanish white in it, if the price require it. The third coat should be ground up in spirits of turpentine only, and diluted with hard varnish, which will dry quick; but should not be applied till the priming be perfectly dry. Of this, probably the seats may require to have two lays, to make the work firm. A very small quantity of turpentine varnish may also be used for cheapness, and to keep the spirit varnish in a more flowing state; but the less it is used the better, since it is of such a quality as makes it very subject to turn soft and clammy by the heat of the body when the chairs are used to sit on; especially, for some time, at their first use. They who use any kind of water colour for rush bottoms, entirely deceive the purchaser, for it rots the rushes, and by the sudden push of the hand upon the seat, the colour will frequently fly off. All the other parts of chairs are primed with Spanish white, and glove leather size, as in any other mode of size painting. Sometimes once over will do, but when the work requires well finishing, three times, which should be rushed, or glass-papered down, for the beauty of the japan depends much upon the well-finished sizing; and it is better when the last coat of sizing is of white lead; upon such a ground, any colour may be laid with advantage, as it will always help the effect of the varnish colours, and particularly bright green and straws.[1]

To shorten the description, the reader should observe that all kinds of colours are to be ground in spirits of turpentine, and no more of it than what is wanted for present use, as it presently dries, and will require as much spirits to grind it as at the first. And the same must be observed in all the varnish colours, and for more reason, for when it is left to stiffen, or set in pots it is entirely wasted.

Of Painting Chairs

In painting chairs with a green ground, common verdigrise may be used; and, as it is extracted from copper, it is of a drying quality, and is much helped in colour by being partly diluted with good turpentine varnish, and partly copal; which will presently dry, if laid on thin, which it always should be. But if, in laying on the last coat of green, the tool be dipped into white hard varnish, in a separate pot, before it is put into the green, this will assist much in speedy drying. The green may be compounded to any shade by means of white lead, and king's yellow, both of which must first be ground in turpentine out of the dry colours.

[1]Notation by author: Early American chairs were not usually given the above-mentioned preparation of whiting and size. Several coats of the foundation or background color were more customary. As the years have passed, we see that the American chairs fared better than the fine English ones done in Sheraton's method, for climatic and temperature changes cause the white grounding to crack and let go, as well as the knocks of ordinary usage. This was particularly noticeable in the case of pieces with a black background.

A straw colour is best compounded of white lead, king's yellow and a little Oxford ochre; and as the king's yellow is a slow drying colour, the more the tint imbibes of this, the more it is requisite to lay it on in white hard varnish. Black grounds for chairs are generally made of lamp black; but the black will bear the best out on a white ground, prepared as before. This colour is of a greasy or oily quality, and a bad drier; consequently, requires a strong size priming. Some burn the lamp black, to take away the oil out of it; but this occasions a great waste, and does not always succeed in drying much sooner. It is sometimes mixed with ivory black, which helps it to dry, but is too dear for common chair work. When cheapness is not so much regarded, it should be ground up in turpentine, very fine, but previously sifted from the grit to which it is subject; and then laid on in white hard varnish, very thin, and repeated. But to help the black, a little varnish composed of asphaltum, black rosin and the drying linseed oil, which was formerly mentioned, may be used in diluting the lamp black, after being ground in turpentine; for observe, lamp black never comes up to its proper colour so well, as when impregnated with something of linseed oil in it. If this asphaltum varnish be used with white lead and lamp black, ground in pure turpentine, it may be applied to chairs as the first priming; and a second, without the white lead, will prepare the chairs for the last coat, which should be in white hard varnish only.

Of Drawing Lines on Chairs

As black chairs look well when ornamented with yellow lines, it may be proper to give some directions as to the mixture of the colour, and the manner of drawing these. King's yellow and white flake, with a trifle of orange lead, ground finely up in spirits of turpentine very thick; for if there be too much of the turpentine, the yellow will wash to the ground, and produce a bad line. After grinding, it should be as a paste, in which state it will admit a proper quantity of copal varnish in diluting it. No other will produce so good a line, and therefore the best of it should be procured as the expence will soon be saved in time. The thickness of this mixture should not be more, when diluted with copal, than will permit it to run freely from the pencil that is filled with it, when pressed against an upright surface; for except it will run from the pencil in such a position, it will not freely leave the pencil when it is pressed on a level surface, which position almost everything is placed in when it is to be run with lines. The kind of pencil should be of camel's hair, very long; some half inch, three quarter, or one inch long in the hair, according to the thickness of the line to be drawn. The pencil being well primed with this colour, which should be kept in a deep hole, bring it to a fine point on a flat marble stone; and in drawing the line, apply the forefinger to some straight angle of the work, and at the same time keeping the pencil between the first finger and the thumb, draw steadily along, and the quicker the better, the line will be drawn, if the colour be in proper order. Any other necessary deviation from this rule, must be learned from experience and practice, which alone can supply the defects of every theory in this art. In ornamenting japanned furniture, no person can proceed further than to do it by line, except he has been previously taught or has practised ornamental drawing himself. To such, a hint or two will be sufficient to enable them to avoid any material error, which I shall point out by some remarks on window and bed cornices, which are generally ornamented with leaves and some kind of trophy, or flowers.

On Japanning Window Cornices

As these do not require a great quantity of Size, I advise only to give one lay of common whiting and size, except on any part that cuts across the grain of the wood, as those with round ends, in which case it will require more sizing with common whiting, that the ground may be rubbed smooth without showing the grain. For if size coats do not hide it, the finishing colours will not. But when the surface of either sort of cornices are smooth and straight, one of size, and the rest in white lead and varnish as before directed; or if two sizings be necessary, let the last be of white lead, if the ground be finished in white; and to preserve the beauty of the white, give it a coat of clear varnish before the ornament is painted upon the ground. If there be any tablet in the center, let this be painted last, that it may not be injured whilst the other parts are finishing.

The ornaments should be sketched in with a black lead pencil very light, and so as not to exceed the outline of the colour. And as the leaves and flowers are proceeded with, they should be nearly finished at the first painting; particularly when the colours are required to dry quick; for in this case the tints will not blend into each other if it be not effected whilst the colours are in some degree wet; and therefore they may be ground up in nut oil, and diluted in copal varnish, which will not set so quick and give more opportunity to retouch the work. When the work is finished thus far, to give it effect, it should be touched with high lights and strong shadows laid quick on, and with colours that will set as quick as may be, to give the greater force, as these things are viewed at a good distance. Thus completed, give the work at least two coats of white hard varnish. But be particular with white grounds, lest any of the soft colours should not be dry, as the varnish is apt to work into such parts, and spoil the ground.

Of Gilding Chairs

This branch of gilding is, in some respects conducted differently from the others in oil and water already mentioned in a previous chapter, though the principles are the same.

The difference is chiefly in point of time, as the chair branch requires the utmost dispatch, that the work may be kept clean, and quickly turned out of hand. Hence the japanner's gold size is of a composition that dries rapidly, and requires the gold to be laid on in the most expert and ready manner. And for this purpose, in narrow fillets, which it chiefly consists of, the leaves of gold may be cut singly, upon a leather cushion with paper under it, and another blank leaf being laid over the gold, and turned over as the narrow strips of gold are laid on, so that the tip for lifting the gold is not wanted, and the work is executed with greater swiftness. It is necessary to begin rather sooner in this than in the other oil gold size, on account of its drying quicker, and it need not be pressed down with cotton until the whole of the chair is covered, and then pass the cotton over the whole. All the japan part of the chair ought to be finished before the gilding be entered upon, that the gold may not be disturbed in the handling, and not merely for this reason, but that the lines or fillets of gold may be trimmed up, by japanning the uneven edges with a colour suitable to the ground, especially if the gilding be any part of it flowered work, for it is impossible to gild the outlines so clean as to require no help by the pencil dipped in the ground colour; and moreover, it should be noticed, that in some cases of small flower and leaf work, it is best to lay on the gold without regard to the outline, and afterwards draw upon the gold, and pick in the ground of the outline. In sizing over for the gold, it should be so coloured as to distinguish the sizing work from the ground of the chair; for the size of itself bears no material colour. A little red lead, vermilion or yellow ochre, will generally do, or if for a dark ground, mix with the size a little white lead. The Japanner's gold size may be made by pulverizing gum animi and asphaltum of each one ounce; red lead, litharge of gold, and umber, of each one ounce and a half, mixing them with a pound of linseed oil and boiling them, observing to stir them until the whole be incorporated, and appear, on growing cold, of the consistence of tar. Strain the mixture through a flannel, and keep it stopped up in a bottle. Another more simple may be made of one pound of linseed oil, four ounces of gum animi; powder the gum, and mix it gradually with the boiling oil. Let it continue to boil, till it be the consistence of tar, and then strain as before.

In gilding chairs with burnished gold, it is not necessary to make the operation as tedious as in picture or glass frame gilding; for the chairs are usually primed in whiting, and the japan laid upon it, forms a base for the gold; it is generally sufficient to give only a coat or two of the bole size and then lay on the gold as in other work. The gold in chair work ought to be varnished to secure it, and the best varnish for this purpose is copal, diluted with a little spirit of turpentine, that it may dry quick, and be more transparent over the gold, which it injures very little when it is thoroughly dry.

A SELECT COLLECTION OF VALUABLE AND CURIOUS ARTS

Fifth Edition—Printed at Concord by William Brown, 1826
Published by Rufus Porter. Copyrighted October 2, 1825

Ornamental Bronze Gilding

This is performed by means of gold or silver reduced to an impalpable powder called bronze. One method of preparing it is, to levigate any quantity of gold or silver leaves on a stone with some clarified honey; dilute the honey with clear water that the bronze may settle; pour off the water and honey and add fresh water to the bronze, which, after being thus thoroughly washed, may be dried on paper, and is ready for use. Another method of preparing the gold bronze is to precipitate the gold from its solution in nitro muriatic acid (see 5) by adding sulphate of iron to the solution;—then washing it, as directed above. But in general it will be found much cheaper to buy the bronze ready prepared.

The ground for this work must be varnished with a mixture of copal varnish with an equal quantity of old linseed oil; and whatever figures are to be formed in bronzing, must be represented by holes cut through pieces of paper. Lay these patterns on the work, when the varnish is so dry as to be but slightly adhesive, but not press them down any more than is requisite to keep the paper in its place. Then take a piece of soft glove leather, moisten it a little by breathing on it, and dip it in some dry bronze, and apply it to the figures beginning at the edges;—tap the figure gently with the leather, and the bronze will stick to the varnish according to the pattern. Thus any figure may be produced in a variety of shades by applying the bronze more freely to some parts of the work than to others. If some internal parts of the figures require to be more distinct than others, they may be wrought by their peculiar patterns, or coloured paint. In some work it may be well to extend the varnish no farther than the intended figures, in which case any projecting or branching parts of the figures, may be drawn with a camel hair pencil, and the pattern may in some measure be dispensed with. In either case, the work must afterwards have one or more coats of copal or shellac varnish.

To enamel picture glasses with gold, the glass must first be washed perfectly clean and dried; then damp it by breathing on it, or wet it with the tongue, and immediately lay on a leaf of gold and brush it down smooth. When this is dry, draw any letters or flowers on the gold with Brunswick blacking (see 51) and when dry, the superfluous gold may be washed off with cotton, leaving the figures entire. Afterward the whole may be covered with blacking or painted in any colour, while the gold figures will appear to advantage on the opposite side of the glass. This work may be elegantly shaded by scratching through the gold with a small steel instrument (in the end of which many sharp points are formed) previous to laying on the blacking. Oil paints of any kind may be substituted in place of the blacking but will not dry so quick.

To write on paper with gold or silver. Make a sizing as strong as will flow freely from the pen, by dissolving equal quantities of gum arabic and loaf sugar in water; write with this on paper and let it dry; then moisten the paper by breathing on it, or by holding it over hot water, and immediately lay pieces of gold or silver leaf on the lines of the writing, pressing them down gently with a dry hair pencil. Otherwise, brush gold or silver bronze lightly over the writing; but this will not have so brilliant an appearance. Allow the sizing to dry again and then brush off the redundant gold or silver with color. This writing, (if performed with leaf gold or silver,) may be burnished with a flint burnisher or a cornelian or blood stone. Gold letters may also be written or drawn with a hair pencil by means of gold bronze, mixed with weak gum water, to which may be added a little solution of soap, which will make it run more freely. But no preparation of solution of gold has yet been discovered which may be easily revived on paper.

Landscape Painting on Walls of Rooms

Dissolve half a pound of glue in a gallon of water, and with this sizing, mix whatever colors may be required for the work. Strike a line round the room nearly breast high; this is called the horizon line: paint the walls from the top to within six inches of the horizon line with sky blue (composed of refined whiting and indigo, or slip blue) and at the same time paint the space from the horizon line to the blue, with horizon red (whiting, coloured a little with orange lead and yellow ochre) and while the two colours are wet, incorporate them partially with a brush. Rising clouds may be represented by striking the horizon red colour upon the blue, before it is dry with a large brush. Change some sky blue about two shades with ship blue and paint your design or rivers, lakes or ocean. Change some sky blue one shade with forest green (ship blue and chrome yellow) and paint the most distant mountains and highlands; shade them while wet, with blue and heighten them with white, observing always to heighten the side that is towards the principal light of the room. The upper surface of the ocean must be painted as high as the horizon line and the distant highlands must rise from ten to twenty inches above it. Paint the highlands, islands, etc., of the second distance, which should appear from four to six miles distant, with mountain green (two parts sky blue with one of forest green,) heighten them, while wet, with sulphur yellow (three parts whiting with one part of chrome yellow) and shade them with blue black, (ship blue and lamp black equal). Paint the lands of the first distance, such as should appear within a mile or two, with forest green; heighten them with chrome yellow and shade with black; occasionally incorporating red ochre, french green or whiting. The nearest part or foreground, however, should be painted very bold with yellow ochre, stone brown, (red and yellow ochres and lamp black equal) and black. Paint the shores and rocks of the first distance with stone brown; heighten with horizon red, shade with black. For those of the second distance, each colour must be mixed with sky blue. The woodlands, hedges and trees of the second distance are formed by striking a small flat brush endwise (which operation is called brushing, and is applied to the heightening and shading all trees and shrubbery of any distance) with mountain green, deepened a little with ship blue; with which also the ground work for trees of the first distance is painted, and with this colour the water may be shaded a little under the capes and islands thus representing the reflection of the land in the water. Trees of the first distance are heightened with sulphur yellow or french green; and shaded with blue black. Every object must be painted larger or smaller according to the distance at which it is represented; thus the proper height of trees in the second distance is from one to two inches, and other objects in proportion. Those in the first distance from six to ten inches generally; but those in the foreground, which are nearest, are frequently painted as large as the walls will admit. The colours also for distant objects, houses, ships, etc., must be varied, being mixed with more or less sky blue, according to the distance of the object. By these means the view will apparently recede from the eye and will have a striking effect.

To Paint in Figures for Carpets or Borders

Take a sheet of pasteboard or strong paper, and paint thereon, with a pencil, any flower or figure that would be elegant for a border of carpet figure; then with small gouges and chissels or a sharp pen knife, cut out the figure completely, that it be represented by apertures cut through the paper. Lay this pattern on the ground intended to receive the figure whether a floor or painted cloth; and with a stiff smooth brush paint with a quick vibrative motion over the whole figure. Then take up the paper and you will have an entire figure on the ground. Note — If a floor is to be thus painted, in imitation of a carpet, the pattern must be perfectly square, and the figure so designed that when several of them come together, they may completely match each other; and when different colours are used in the same figure, they must be kept a little separate from each other, and wrought with different brushes.

To Paint in Imitation of Mahogany and Maple

First give the work one or two coats of straw coloured paint, composed of white lead and yellow ochre, ground in linseed oil, to which may be added a little fine letharge, that the paint may the sooner dry; when this is dry, rub it smooth with sand paper. Then if mahogany is to be imitated, stain the work over with boiled linseed oil; coloured a little with venetian red and burnt terra-de-sienna, equal quantities. This should be applied with a short stiff brush, and spread very thin, that it may not run or drip off. Then with terra-de-sienna, ground very thick in oil form the dark shades of the graining according to your design with a small flat brush. For this purpose a common sash-brush may be made flat, by having a small piece of wire, or wood, bound on each side near the handle. Some of the darker shades may be drawn with burnt umber and black ground together, which may be applied with a camel hair pencil. If any part is to be made very light the staining may be wiped off carefully with a ball of cotton. Light stripes or lines may be produced by drawing a piece of cork or soft wood over the work, thus taking off or removing the dark colours, that the original ground may appear. To imitate maple, the work must be stained with yellow ochre and burnt umber and ground together in linseed oil. Instead of burnt umber, terra-de-sienna (unburnt) is sometimes used, but as different kinds or parcels of it vary in colour, from yellow to brown, it may not be depended on uniformly. The birds-eyes and curls are formed by removing the staining from the ground with a piece of stiff leather, the edges of which are cut in notches, so that the several points will touch the work at the same time.

To Give Tin a Changeable Crystalline Appearance

Cleanse the tin by washing it with warm soap and water and rinse it in clear water. Then heat the tin to the temperature of bare sufferance to the hand, and pour on it or apply with a brush or sponge, a mixture of one ounce of muriatic acid with one fourth of an ounce of sulphuric acid, and two ounces of water; then immediately wash the tin in clear water. Another method is to apply in the same manner a solution of two ounces of muriate of soda, in four ounces of water, with one ounce of nitric acid. In either case, if the crystalline figures are not bold enough, the operation may be repeated. If a very small figure is required, the tin may be heated nearly to glowing and plunged into cold water, slightly acidulated with nitric and muriatic acids. If a little solder is drawn over the tin with a hot iron or copper, in such a manner as to form a cross or circle, and the opposite side of the tin be afterward crystalized, it will have a beautiful effect.

To Make a Gold Coloured Varnish for Tin

To half a pint of alcohol in a flask add one ounce of gum-shellac and half an ounce of turmeric both in powder; set the flask in a warm place frequently shaking it for twelve hours or more; then filter or strain off the liquor which may be occasionally diluted with new rum. If a colour is required resembling dutch gold, a small quantity of dragons blood may be added or substituted in place of turmeric. When this varnish is used it must be applied to the work freely and flowing and must not be brushed or rubbed while it is drying. One or more coats of varnish (or lacquer as it is sometimes called) may be laid on the work as the colour is required deeper or lighter. Note — To make a rose-coloured varnish, proceed as above directed, only substitute one fourth of an ounce of the best lake, finely ground in the place of turmeric. A transparent blue varnish may also be made by means of prussian blue; and purple or green by adding a little blue to the gold or rose coloured varnishes. These lacquers are frequently employed for washing silver bronzed ornaments to give them the appearance of gold or copper.

Brunswick Blacking for Picture Glasses

Take one pound of gum asphaltum and melt it over a slow fire; then take it from the fire and add spirits of turpentine in small quantities, stirring it briskly until it is of the consistence of varnish. When it is nearly cold, strain it through a flannel, and bottle it for use. This blacking is used for bordering picture glasses, and is probably the most perfect black in nature. It is water proof and dries very quick.

To Make a Print Appear on a Gold Ground

Dilute veneer turpentine with spirits of turpentine till it works freely with a camel hair pencil; lay a coat of this varnish on any part of a print or picture observing to keep the pencil within the lines that the varnish may not spread beyond. Then lay a coat of the varnish on the same part of the back of the paper, and lay on a leaf of gold over the varnished part, press down the gold very gently with cotton and the varnish having rendered the paper transparent, the face of the picture will appear as if those parts were printed in gold. By this varnish, which is less liable to spread in the paper than oil, pictures may be so prepared that the colours of various parts of them may be varied and changed at pleasure by placing pieces of silk or paper of different colours on the back of them.

GOODRICH & THOMPSON BOOK

Receipt for Making Japanned Varnish

To 1 Gallon of Linseed Oil
To 1 lb. Gum Asphaltum
To 1½ lb. Rosin
To ½ lb. Gum Shallack
To 1½ lb. Umber. Pound the Umber fine.

To 3 Gallons of oil you want a 14 Gallon Iron Kettle. Put in the oil and then apply the other ingredients. Make a good fire under the pot. After it boils one hour or more it will rise if it is like to boil over, stir it and quench the fire — if it boils over cover it with a piece of sheet iron and that will stop it. It will more or less for about two hours then it will go down. Then keep a moderate fire under the pot. Try it by sticking a strip of tin into it. When it is boiled enough it will be so hard that you can hardly stir it when it is on the tin. Let it get middling cool then add 1 gallon of spirits of turpentine to 1 gallon of oil if that does not thin it enough put in a little more. Let it settle two or three days before using it. Boil sometimes 3 or 4 hours after it goes down. Take a pleasant day to make the varnish.

For Making Blacking for Tin Ware

To 1 Pint Spirits of Turpentine add ½ lb. Lamp Black
To 1 Pint Copal Varnish, ½ pt. Japanned Varnish

Bronzing —

The bronzing is done by patterns cut out of paper and laid onto the article to be bronzed put on a thin coat of varnish (the Japanned Varnish reduced) let it stand until it will stick a little then apply the bronze over the paper where the figures are cut with a rag with cotton wool tied up then take off the paper let it stand till the varnish is dry then varnish over the whole with Copal varnish. Good bronze is wourth about 7/6 an oz two colours.

To Make Gold Coloured Varnish for Tin

To half Pint Alcohol in a flask add one ounce of gum Shelac, half an ounce of tumeric, and one fourth ounce of red saunders. Set the flask in warm place frequently shaking it for 12 hours or more. Then filter or strain off the liquor which may be occasionally reduced with alcohol. If a colour is required resembling Dutch Gold or copper, a large proportion of the red Saunders may be used. When this varnish is used it must be applied to the work freely and flowing, and must not be brushed or rubbed while drying. One or more coats of this varnish or lacquer as it is sometimes called may be laid on the work as the colour is required to be deeper or lighter. To make a rose coloured varnish proceed as above only substitute ¼ of an ounce of Lake finely ground in the place of tumeric. A transparent blue varnish may be also made by means of Prussian blue and purple or green by adding a little blue to the gold or rose coloured varnishes.

INDEX